DECORATIVE AMERICAN
POTTERY
& WHITEWARE

IDENTIFICATION AND VALUE GUIDE

Jeanie Klamm Wilby

COLLECTOR BOOKS
A Division of Schroeder Publishing Co., Inc.

On the Cover

Back Row:
Steubenville Pottery Co. (Flow Blue portrait plate)
Taylor, Smith & Taylor Co. (tankard with monk)
Anchor Pottery Co. (platter with fish)

Middle Row
East Liverpool Pottery Co. (pitcher with portrait)
Smith-Phillips China Co. (souvenir portrait plate)
Dresden Pottery (lemonade pitcher and cup)

Front Row
Knowles, Taylor & Knowles Co. (plate with roses)

Cover design: Beth Summers
Book design: Joyce Cherry

Collector Books
P.O. Box 3009
Paducah, KY 42002-3009

www.collectorbooks.com

Searching For A Publisher?

We are always looking for people knowledgeable within their fields. If you feel that there is a real need for a book on your collectible subject and have a large comprehensive collection, contact Collector Books.

The current values in this book should be used only as a guide. They are not intended to set prices, which vary from one section of the country to another. Auction prices as well as dealer prices vary greatly and are affected by condition and demand. Neither the author nor the publisher assumes responsibility for any losses which might be incurred as a result of consulting this guide.

Contents

Acknowledgments

This book is the result of my desire to share beautiful pottery with new collectors. Many pottery collectors focus on pricey art pottery and porcelain and overlook this genre of the industry, so it is my hope to document many of the pieces our families have treasured over the years and help others learn more about their history.

I've seen beautiful pieces of pottery from around the world and value all, but none like those pieces American made. I share this appreciation with my friend Faye Lyon, who encouraged me to "write a book"; the idea would never have occurred to me without her prodding. When my husband, Tom, began telling people I was writing a book, there was no turning back.

My thanks to the members of the East Liverpool Pottery Collectors who were always available to answer questions and point me in the right direction. Special thanks to James L. Murphy, Professor, Ohio State University Libraries, Columbus, Ohio, for going way out of his way to help me research Clarus Ware. I'm grateful to the many people along the way who answered hundreds of little questions and listened attentively when I would ramble on and on about a piece and its history — Thomas and Trevor know exactly what I mean.

Most importantly, thanks to my husband, Tom, who took all the photos, kept the computer running, and kept me on track. This is his book as much as mine.

Introduction

A few years ago, while browsing in a bookstore, I picked up a copy of Jo Cunningham's book *An Encyclopedia of American Dinnerware*. As I looked through the pages, I saw the familiar patterns of my parents' and grandparents' dinnerware and was amazed that anyone cared enough about this "old stuff" to write a book.

After realizing I had several of these patterns in my own cabinet, I began frequenting yard sales and thrift stores to see what else I could find. One piece at a time, I began accumulating anything that seemed old (50+ years) and American made. My husband and I were in the middle of a year-long cross-country trip in an RV, so it was really not the best time to gather heavy, breakable china, but it was a great time to learn. With the help of a few reference books, I became fascinated with an American industry I hadn't even realized existed.

As I learned about the history of the pottery industry and discovered the variety of beautiful items produced in America, I became hooked on collecting. From American dinnerware, I migrated to American decorative pieces, and now enjoy finding moderately priced decorative pottery made around the turn of the century.

There are so many American potteries that produced beautiful decorative pieces, how does one ever narrow down a selection for a book? I have chosen items that are reasonably priced and easy to find with a little hunting and patience. That leaves out many spectacular examples of early wares, but does leave lots of material for future books. Maybe yours.

This book was written to introduce the fun of collecting decorative pottery that was made by American pottery companies in the early twentieth century. It concentrates on lovely, reasonably priced items that can be found in antique shops, garage sales, flea markets, and online auctions. By sharing samples of my collection, I hope to inspire the reader to begin his or her own collection. Chances are, you have a piece that was your grandmother's (or great-grandmother's) somewhere around the house. Check the mark on the bottom. You may have already started your collection.

This collection is by no means complete. Hundreds of American potteries produced thousands of decorative pieces. The collection presented in this book is a fraction of what is available, so undoubtedly someone will be disappointed that his or her favorite pottery was not represented. A collection is a work in progress, so can one ever hope to obtain samples of every pottery? Probably not, but that desire keeps us collecting!

Why American?

I happened to mention to a friend from another country that I was collecting American pottery. He had to stifle a laugh when he realized I was serious. While a few American potteries' wares are highly sought after, the majority often "get no respect." Pottery produced in America has differed immensely in quality due to causes ranging from clay composition and firing techniques to the art of the decorator, and there are wonderful success stories in the history of American pottery. In fact, several companies made fine belleek and porcelain wares, while others made semi-porcelain vases that have beautiful glazes and are highly prized. Today, these gorgeous pieces bring hundreds and thousands of dollars. But most American potteries also produced decorative china that is mostly overlooked by serious collectors worldwide. This genre of the pottery industry varied in quality over the years, and with those variations you have part of the history of American pottery making. Though most American collectors seem to concentrate on fine porcelain, art china, or nostalgic dinnerware, these decorative pieces tell their own story of America and its development, the history of each company and its employees, and the evolution of personal styles and tastes. What tales that one-hundred-year-old vase on the piano could tell. Who before me cherished the lovely floral plate hanging on the wall?

We have the opportunity to rediscover these treasures and possess them ourselves before handing them over to the next generation of collectors, who will also wonder at their history. Alice Morse Earle described this love of collecting in an 1891 article titled "A China Hunter in New England." She wrote, "Insight into human nature — love of my native country — knowledge of her natural beauties — acquaintance with her old landmarks and historical localities — familiarity with her history — admiration of her noble military and naval heroes — and study of the ancient manners, customs, and traditions of her early inhabitants have all been fostered, strengthened, and indeed almost brought into existence, by the search after and study of old china."

As you look through this book and discover the charm and beauty of what American potters created, you can't help but take pride in their efforts. Their wares represent America's heritage.

Understanding Pottery

To some, the term "pottery" may mean a terracotta pot or stoneware crock. To others, it is any ware made from clay. What is added to the clay, how it is glazed and decorated, and how it is fired makes the difference between a 59-cent pot at Wal-Mart and a $5000 Lotus Ware vase by Knowles, Taylor & Knowles. Clay mixed with water becomes pliable and holds its shape when dried. When heated it becomes hard and durable. When glazed it becomes waterproof. The differences between terra cotta and porcelain are the result of different types of clay, additives, glazes, and firing techniques.

Three major types of pottery are earthenware, stoneware, and porcelain. Earthenware is fired at a low temperature. It is relatively porous (will absorb water) and not very strong, and is therefore usually heavier than other pottery and less expensive to produce. When glazed, it becomes waterproof and can be used in the kitchen. Terra cotta and red ware are earthenwares made with red clay.

Stoneware is fired at a higher temperature and is non-porous (won't absorb water), even without glaze. It is stronger than earthenware, but not translucent.

Porcelain, which contains kaolin and petuntse, is fired at very high temperatures, making it translucent, strong, and non-porous.

American potteries made all types of pottery. Earthenware and stoneware made in the early years of production in America tended to be utilitarian, and potters continually strove to produce finer wares. Struggling to perfect porcelain techniques, American companies often imported European potters. As the quality of their wares improved, they began making decorative porcelain and semi-porcelain wares to compete with the European market.

Stoneware syrup pitcher made by Knowles, Taylor & Knowles.

By the late nineteeth century, many American potteries had progressed to making whiteware, a fine grade of white or nearly white earthenware that could be highly decorated and fired to a vitreous or semi-vitreous state. Vitreous wares are those that are nearly as non-porous as glass; semi-vitreous wares are somewhat more porous. (The degree of porosity can be determined by submersing an item in water and determining the amount of water it absorbs. Today, the Federal Government sets standards for items to be called vitreous.)

As whiteware techniques improved, American potteries were able to produce very decorative pieces that could compete with more expensive porcelain wares. In fact, many companies

Earthenware bowl made by Watt Pottery.

Porcelain demitasse cup made by Willets Manufacturing Co.

producing semi-porcelain used the term "porcelain" in their marks, since the wares had the look of porcelain. Today, it is common for the non-collector to use the terms "china" and "porcelain" to describe wares that appear to be of quality, though they may not actually meet the precise definition. Therefore, when you see an item in a shop described as "porcelain" or "china" (or even "ceramic"), it may very well be whiteware.

If these descriptions are confusing to you, you are not alone. I do not waste time vexing over whether an item is vitreous, semi-vitreous, porcelain, semi-porcelain, china, fine earthenware, stoneware, etc. I agree with the sentiment Edwin Atlee Barber expressed in his book *The Pottery and Porcelain of The United States* (Third Edition, 1909), when he wrote, "If the object under consideration possesses genuine beauty of form, or real merit in the decoration which has been placed upon it; if it has historical value, or represents some particular phase in the ceramic development of any country or locality, it loses none of its interest because the owner or the practical potter is unable to decide in which group to place it."

American Potteries

Potteries evolve where desirable clay deposits are found. It is believed that primitive American potteries were producing as early as the mid-1600s in the New Jersey and New York regions, and there are records of potteries operating by the mid-1700s. By the mid-1800s, Trenton, New Jersey, and East Liverpool, Ohio, had become leaders in production due to rich clay deposits in their respective areas.

American potteries struggled to perfect their techniques and encountered many problems. There are many things that can go wrong in the production of pottery, especially in the glazing and firing processes, and it was not unusual to lose entire kilns of pottery. Pottery making of this era was labor intensive and depended on more costly, skilled labor. Management was often involved in bitter disputes with labor unions, and strikes were not uncommon. In addition, struggling potteries had to overcome the widespread belief in the superiority of European pottery, especially English wares. In fact, the English potters dominated the American pottery market until the Morrill Tariff of 1861. The tariff opened the door for American wares to compete

The Taylor, Smith & Taylor Co. plant in Chester, West Virginia (across the
Ohio River from East Liverpool, Ohio).

8

with the imports, and many new potteries were built. Soon afterward, according to an article by Carrie M. Hawley in *The Midland Monthly,* July 1894, "Potteries at last began to spring up so rapidly that in 1881 there were eight hundred in operation in the United States. East Liverpool has become the great center, having twenty-nine potteries, nine decorating works, two still and triangle factories, one sagger factory and three for the making of door knobs. Millions of dollars

Ad for Homer Laughlin featuring the American eagle over the British lion backstamp.

worth are manufactured here every year, from the yellow and Rockingham wares to some of our choicest productions." The author further relates, "Trenton, N.J., the 'Staffordshire of America,' has invested nearly three millions in the manufacture of crockery and china, and fully six thousand men, women, and children here find steady and remunerative employment."

As American potteries improved their wares, there was a movement to acknowledge and pay tribute to the quality of American pottery. Though many companies chose to name their potteries after European companies like Dresden and Sevres, perhaps hoping to confuse their customers, some companies chose to flaunt their successes. One such company was Homer Laughlin, who as early as 1877 used the mark of an eagle over a prostrate lion on its china. This was meant to imply the superiority of the American eagle over the British lion.

But old habits die hard, and it wasn't until 1917 that an American company, Lenox, was chosen by President Woodrow Wilson as the official provider of White House china, breaking with a long tradition of using European china. The market for Amercan made pottery was further helped by World War I, which blocked the import of many goods to this country. After the war, there was a rush of patriotism and a desire to buy American. Mass production and decorating techniques had improved, including the development of easy-to-apply decals. Many American potteries flourished, especially those that kept up with the ever-changing American tastes. By the 1940s, Americans were happy with American dinnerware, but by the 1950s things had changed. New materials like plastic were becoming popular (anyone remember Melmanine?), and imports became more economical to the buyer. Customers flocked to the low-priced Japanese import market, and soon American companies started closing their doors. Only a few of the large potteries operate today.

Marks

This is the fun part. I never tire of researching a mark or discovering one I've never seen before. I've been known to buy a piece just so I could look up the mark! When you start collecting, it is very easy to get confused. The "mark" or "backstamp" is simply the name or symbol of the maker. Potteries usually marked their wares on the backside or bottom with a stamp of the pottery. Marks may be under or over the glaze, they may be impressed or raised, and sometimes a company used a paper label. The marks may indicate the name of the pottery, the shape or pattern of the item, the date it was made, and often the plant where it was produced.

Many companies used a variety of marks. The different marks may serve to identify a particular style or line. Marks often changed as a result of some type of structural or name change within the company. Because of the problems and high costs of operating a pottery, many companies came in and out of business quite often. It was not uncommon for a pottery to run into financial trouble, reorganize, change names, merge with another pottery, or all of the above. If we know what mark a company used at a particular time, we can identify the pottery an item came from and determine its age.

While most potteries producing decorative wares had some system for marking their wares, many pieces were missed. Since many companies used the same decals, it is very difficult to know the origin of a piece unless it is marked.

One clue used in dating pottery is available as a result of the McKinley Tariff Act passed by Congress in 1890. This legislation not only increased tariffs on foreign goods, but also required all imported pottery to be marked with the country of origin. Remember, however, many foreign pieces not made for export found their way here. Another clue to orgin and date would be what's included in the mark. The words "Made in U.S.A." were not used in marks prior to 1920, so that would tell you your piece is post-1920.

So, start to put the pieces of the puzzle together. Once you get hooked, I strongly recommend the two books that are the most comprehensive. The first is *DeBolt's Dictionary of American Pottery Marks*. This book is the "bible," because it not only shows marks but also gives approximate time periods of manufacture. You should also have *Lehner's Encyclopedia of U.S. Marks on Pottery, Porcelain and Clay*. It contains a wealth of information about the history of American potteries. I can't tell you how many times I've gone through these books page by page.

The more you learn, the more likely you are to find errors in your pottery reference books. As most of these potteries no longer exist and records are long gone, we must do our own detective work. Sometimes marks are attributed to the wrong company and the error passes from one author to another, and perhaps someone will find that I have perpetuated one of these errors. I welcome such information and the chance to find the rightful home of a misrepresented piece of pottery. There are still a lot of mysteries out there.

This mark was used by Taylor, Smith & Taylor from about 1910 to about 1915.

This mark was used by Taylor, Smith & Taylor from about 1908 to about 1915.

Decorating

Transfer Printing

Transfer printing was a boon to pottery production. By 1756, workers could ink an engraved copper plate and transfer the design to tissue paper. Applying the tissue paper to the piece of pottery would leave the design on the surface, which sure beat hand painting and meant decorated pottery could be turned out at a faster rate. Often a transfer was accented with hand painting.

Decals

The word "decal" is a shortened form of the French word "decalcomania," which refers to transferring a pattern or design by applying pressure, but in the case of decorating pottery, a decal would be applied to an item with varnish, to hold it in place; the backing would then be saturated and removed. Decals were first used in Europe in the 1800s, and by the turn of the century they were being imported into America. They were applied by hand until nearly the 1940s, when they became commonly applied by machine.

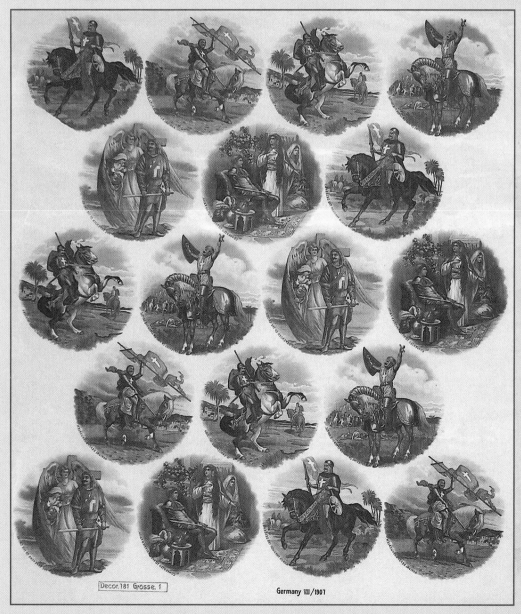

Sheet of decals imported from Germany, dated 1907. This series was used by Knowles, Taylor & Knowles.

This Crusade series decal appears on plates made by Knowles, Taylor & Knowles.

Many American potteries used foreign-made decals, and it is not unusual to see the same decal on wares of different companies and sometimes — on wares of different countries. That is also why, unless a piece is marked, it is hard to tell who actually made it. Wildlife decals designed by artists such as R. K. Beck, for example, were used by many companies. Often the artist's signature is incorporated in the decal.

Two game plates with the same decal by R.K. Beck.

Crescent China.

French China Co.

Queen Louise portrait decals were also used by many companies, so you must rely on the backstamp to determine maker.

Smith-Phillips China Co.

Globe Pottery Co.

Ohio China Co. Imperial

Ohio China Co. Limoges

Defining The Collection

Through the late 1800s and early 1900s, American potteries experienced great successes and great failures. World-class porcelain and belleek were produced in America and are still highly prized today. Art pottery with hand painting and beautiful glazes was produced, and brings unbelievable prices in today's market. In fact, there were so many spectacular wares produced that it is hard to limit your collecting to one company or one type of pottery. When I started collecting I was drawn to the dinnerware and kitchenware you might remembered seeing at your grandmother's. Over time, I became fascinated with the decorative pottery that was produced around the turn of the century. I found that even though these lovely pieces are from eighty to over one hundred years old, they are reasonably priced and not hard to find. Decorative pieces from this era make up the collection in this book and are further defined below.

Decorative

Many pottery companies made their living selling dinnerware but also produced specialty wares, which today we like to call "cabinet plates," or as noted in the 1908 Sears, Roebuck & Co. catalogue, "rail plates." These specialty pieces may have included highly decorated wares meant only for display, or more functional items like cake plates or pitchers that weren't part of a dinnerware set. By today's standards, some of these pieces are so lovely you wouldn't dream of serving food on them. Instead, you would display them. This book focuses on decorative items from around the turn of the century through the 1920s. While I collectively call these pieces "decorative," I use the term loosely, as in their day, many were meant to be used.

Availability

I've included pieces that are often available through antique shops, online storefronts, and auctions. Once you know what you are looking for and if you have a bit of patience, you will find them everywhere. I have found beautiful pieces in wonderful condition at yard sales, flea markets, thrift stores, auctions, rummage sales, and especially online. The online auctions are a marvelous source for obtaining beautiful pieces for your collection, and a fantastic classroom for learning about them. Where else can you look at literally thousands of marks and patterns in a sitting? Also, online are hundreds of storefronts. That is where the seller lists, at fixed prices, the items he or she wants to sell. If you are serious about collecting, you'll love having a computer to help you shop.

I have identified pieces in this book by their mark. If you find you are drawn to wares with a particular mark, I encourage you to pick up a book on marks and learn the other marks used by the same pottery, so you can expand your collection.

Cost and Pricing

Another criteria for this collection is cost. Most pieces chosen are reasonably priced under $150. In many cases, these wares can be obtained for under $50 and with luck, you may do even better. As you can imagine, values are difficult to set, and the ones given here are only meant to be a guide. They have been determined from pricing obtained at antique shops, pricing guidebooks, online auctions, and antique shows. Since few of the pieces in this collection are one-of-a-kind, highest prices as well as very low prices were disregarded. Prices are meant to reflect what you would fairly expect to pay for the same item in very good condition in an antique shop. Some patterns are more desirable than others and often bring higher prices. Collectors like all sorts of things such as portraits, cherubs, roses, and certain animals like bears or bunnies or the ever popular bluebirds. Calendar and advertising pieces bring higher prices, as does on Flow Blue. So, if you have a Flow Blue calendar plate with advertising and bluebirds, you'll have numerous collectors fighting over it and hence, a higher value. Bear in mind that some parts of the country value certain marks more than others, so there will certainly be some variance.

Online auctions have caused a bit of confusion for pottery collectors. Generally, auction prices are considered to be wholesale values, but sometime retail values are paid for desirable items. On the other hand, you can sometimes find a great bargain because the seller did not recognize on item's value or listed an item incorrectly. Also, when considering online auction prices, you must take into account shipping, insurance, and risk.

In a fast growing market like pottery collecting, you cannot rely on a price guide to be the final word. You must do your own homework and decide what the item is worth to you.

Condition

If you like it and you want it, buy it! You'll find pottery, like other collectible items, continues to increase in value. To protect your investment, there are some basic rules for collecting that will serve you well.

Unless it is rare, try to avoid buying items with chips or cracks. A crack is a crack and no matter how fine (hairline) it is, it will eventually affect the integrity of the item. A chip on the back, where it is not seen, may be acceptable to you, but it still affects the overall value of the piece. Chips and cracks can be repaired, but doing so is costly and may exceed the value of the item. Be patient, often the same damaged piece you were tempted to buy will come along again with no damage (and sometimes cheaper).

Most of the pieces in this category have crazing. Crazing is the name for fine lines in the glaze, and is due to stress between the glaze and the body. When the body and glaze expand and contract at different rates, the outcome is crazing. This is often a result of the glazing and firing processes and is not necessarily related to the age of an item. I don't mind crazing at all on decorative pieces, and if you believe what you read on many eBay auctions, others seem to agree. "The crazing adds to its beauty." If you don't like crazing, you are in the wrong category of collecting.

Some pieces are darkened or stained to the point you cannot appreciate the design. There are ways to clean china (see Care and Cleaning, next page), but they add cost and inconvenience. If you don't clean china, you may want to pass on a badly stained item.

Hairline crack, may not go through.

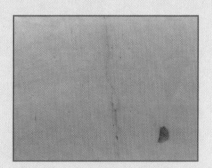

Crack, can be felt with fingernail and goes through.

Small chip, commonly called a flea-bite (approx. 1/16").

Chip, not a flea-bite

Here, the even crazing adds allure to the picture.

Care and Cleaning

Wash dishes carefully with dish detergent and warm water and dry gently. If allowed to air dry, your dishes may have water spots, so it helps to wipe them with a soft paper towel. For hard to reach or embossed areas, you can use a soft-bristled toothbrush and baking soda or Bon Ami™. I have read where people recommend bleaching an item to remove staining. PLEASE DON'T BLEACH! I REPEAT, NEVER USE HOUSEHOLD BLEACH TO CLEAN CHINA. I don't care who told you it works, it will ruin your china. It may appear to work fine at first, but over time it erodes the finish, and you will see the glaze start to flake. Perhaps you have seen a piece of china in a shop with some areas of glaze starting to separate, or what looks like tiny salt crystals forming on the glaze. This is the effect of household bleach.

Platter before hydrogen peroxide treatment.

Professionals use hydrogen peroxide of at least 30% strength to remove staining. Hydrogen peroxide attacks organic (food) matter under the glaze and allows it to bleed out. One method is to soak cotton strips in the hydrogen peroxide and then wrap the cotton around the item. Completely wrap with plastic wrap and set aside for several days. When you unwrap, you'll see the cotton has absorbed the yellowish looking organic matter (it looks like yellow oil) from the plate. You may need to repeat this procedure several times. When the cotton no longer turns yellow, place the item in the sun or in the oven at a temperature no higher than 150° F for about an hour. This will force out any remaining organic matter and get rid of any residual chemical. (Note: Some people claim higher temperatures will cause crazing. I use 170° F because that is the lowest temperature my oven will heat, and I have not noticed any damage.) The item must then be allowed to dry out completely before use or it will damage any surface upon which it is placed. (Ask me about my kitchen counter.)

Platter cleaned with hydrogen peroxide method described.

Another method of cleaning is to simply soak the item in an open hydrogen peroxide bath rather than wrapping it in cotton, and then follow the same heating procedure as above. This method requires the need for a work area that will not be disturbed by kids or pets.

Hydrogen peroxide is a dangerous chemical, and care is needed when using either method. Most people purchase hydrogen peroxide at beauty supply stores.

Please read all directions and cautions associated with this caustic chemical, which can even be explosive if not handled properly. Rubber gloves must be used when working with with hydrogen peroxide.

I have used hydrogen peroxide on many pieces of the type covered in this book and have had great success, but I am not an expert in chemicals and pottery so I cannot guarantee you the same results. Please use this cleaning process at your own risk; hopefully, you will have good results also.

There may be those who object to cleaning pottery and prefer the aged look. Since this aged look is acquired from food particles and handling, I have not personally met anyone who does not appreciate a clean, more sanitary look, but this is something you must decide for yourself.

Coffee filters placed between your plates help protect them from rubbing. Coffee filters come in several sizes, and I use them all. I especially like the oversized ones which can be found at restaurant supply or office supply stores. All are very inexpensive and will protect your plates from scrapes and scratches.

Coffee filters separating plates.

Coffee filters, size 7", 8", and 9½".

When I display a piece of china on a table, like a vase, the first thing I do is put small felt stick-on pads on the bottom. This not only protects my table, but it protects the vase from chipping as it is picked up and put down. Lids get the same treatment. You can find these pads in all sizes at home improvement stores.

Pads on base of item to protect item and table.

Pads on lid help protect the piece from chips.

Hanging your plates with a wire hanger is fine if you take some care. Some people recommend only brass hangers, but I find that you can use any kind if you make some adjustments. You may have seen plates with chips or rust caused by hangers. To avoid this, keep the tension on the spring just tight enough to hold the plate and no tighter. Find some clear plastic tubing (aquarium supply) and cover the ends of the hanger where it wraps around the plate. And, just to be safe, put a paper plate between the back of the plate and the hanger so no metal touches the plate. You can also coat the ends of the wire hanger with a product called Plasti Dip™, which comes in clear and white and will protect your plate from touching metal. If you are using a metal plate rack to display your china, you can slit a piece of tubing lengthwise and position it over the rack where your plate rests.

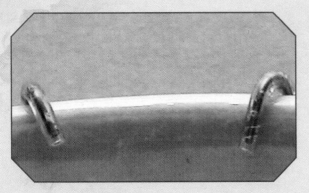

Clear tubing on ends

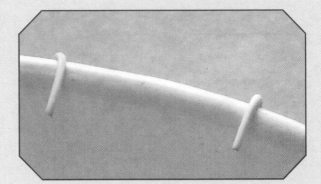

White Plasti Dip™

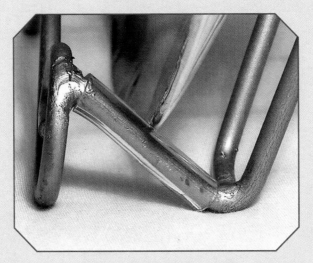

Clear tubing on plate holder.

One more tip: try to avoid picking up an old piece of china by the handle (especially when you are in an antique shop). The less stress on that part, the better. With luck and care, those old pieces will be around to delight future generations.

The Collection

Akron China Company

The Akron China Co., of Akron, Ohio, was in operation from 1894 to 1908. It used several marks in its short life, and this mark is the one most often found. Notice the lettering of *ACCo* in the center.

This mark was used from about 1898 to about 1905. Reads "REVERE CHINA AKRON OHIO." (Mark retouched for clarity.)

Plate (7½") with cherub design, green trim, and embossing around the border. $45.00 – 55.00

American China Company

The American China Co. opened in Toronto, Ohio, in 1897 and closed around 1910. It produced good quality semi-porcelain and whiteware. Though this company was only in business for a short time, its pieces can still be found with a little effort, and some are very highly decorated.

This mark was used from about 1905 to about 1910.

Plate (10") with floral design and gold trim. $35.00 – 45.00.

Plate (9½") with floral design and gold trim.
$35.00 – 45.00.

Plate (10") with water lilies and green trim.
$35.00 – 45.00.

Pitcher (6½") with roses and orange lustre.
$55.00 – 65.00.

Pitcher (6½″) with roses and green lustre.
$55.00 – 65.00.

This mark was used from about 1905 to about 1910.
Reads "AMERICAN CHINA CO., TORONTO,
OHIO, U.S.A." (Mark retouched for clarity.)

Pitcher (10½″) with cherries. $125.00 – 145.00.

*I could not find a reference for this mark, so I suspect
it is not common. Because it incorporates U.S.A. like
the two previous marks, I would place it from
about 1905 to 1910.*

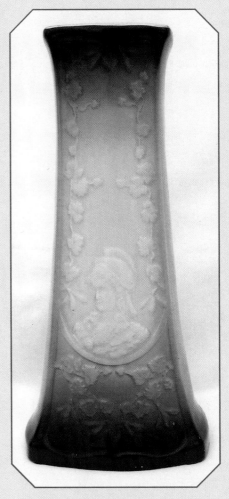

*Portrait vase (12"). Same decal as found
on the Warwick pieces. $175.00 – 195.00.*

Back view.

Anchor Pottery Company

The Anchor Pottery Company, of Trenton, New Jersey, was founded by James E. Norris in 1894 and was in operation until the mid-1920s.

This mark was used from about 1904 to about 1912.

Plate (10") with embossing around the rim.
$30.00 – 40.00.

Pitcher (8½") with flowers and pink border.
$75.00 – 85.00.

*Fish platter (14" x 10"), probably part of a fish set. Decal includes
signature of artist, R. K. Beck. $75.00 – 85.00.*

*A variation of the previous mark. The initials JEN are
for the founder, J.E. Norris.*

*Bowl (9¾") with grapes.
$20.00 – 30.00.*

The Bennett Pottery Company operated in Baltimore, Maryland, from 1846 to 1936 and produced good quality wares.

This mark was used from about 1890 to about 1897.
Reads "Alba China."

Mug (5″) with coat of arms.
$45.00 – 55.00.

Side view.

William Brunt Pottery Company

The Brunt family had a long history in American pottery, starting as early as the mid-1800s. This leg of the company is believed to have started around 1892, in East Liverpool, Ohio, and it operated until about 1911. The company produced many decorative pieces.

This mark was used from about 1900 to 1911. Notice the similarity to the Knowles, Taylor & Knowles mark.

Plate (8½″) with strawberries.
$35.00 – 45.00.

Plate (9″) with roses. Decal incorporates artist's signature, Guyeau. $35.00 – 45.00.

This mark was used from about 1892 to 1911.

Bowl (11") with elaborate embossing.
$45.00 – 55.00.

Plate (6") with roses. $20.00 – 30.00.
From the collection of Faye Lyon.

Plate (6") with fruit. $20.00 – 30.00.
From the collection of Faye Lyon.

Plate (6") with fruit and roses. $20.00 – 30.00.
From the collection of Faye Lyon.

This mark was used from about 1900 to 1911.

Plate (10") with figural scene. $65.00 – 75.00.

Buffalo Pottery

Buffalo Pottery was formed in 1901, in Buffalo, NY, and started production in 1903, making semi-vitreous ware. Buffalo Pottery is well known for its line of Blue Willow (Old Willow), historical and commemorative decorations, advertising pieces, Abino Ware, and its famous Deldare Ware. The Deldare Ware line features hand-painted Old English scenes and is highly sought after and therefore quite expensive. In 1915, the company started producing a line of institutional ware with the Buffalo China backstamp, and in 1956, changed its name to the Buffalo China Company. Buffalo China is still in operation today as a division of Oneida, Ltd.

This mark is found on game plates and usually includes the date. Note: 1907 is the year given in this instance.

Game plate (9¼") dated 1908. Front reads "WILD DUCKS." $65.00 – 75.00.

Game plate (9¼"), date incomplete. Front reads "WILD TURKEYS." $65.00 – 75.00.

Game plate (9¼"), dated 1907. Front reads "AMERICAN HERRING GULL." $65.00 – 75.00.

Though I could not get an exact reference for this mark, it was most likely used from about 1903 to no later than 1915. I believe the following plate was made from about 1905 to about 1911. (Mark retouched for clarity.)

Plate (9¼") with roses. $60.00 – 70.00.

I would estimate this mark was used from about 1905 to about 1915.

Plate (7½") with Niagara Falls view. $65.00 – 75.00.

Burford Brothers Pottery Company

Burford Brothers Pottery operated from 1879 to 1904, in East Liverpool, Ohio, and often used the term "porcelain" in its mark, even on wares that were actually semi-porcelain.

This mark was used from about 1900 to 1904. Companies often used the term "porcelain" in their marks, even when their wares were actually semi-porcelain.

Platter (13½" x 7") with flowers.
$40.00 – 50.00.

Plate (7") with couple. Reads
"IT'S UP TO YOU." $20.00 – 30.00.

Burroghs & Mountford Company

Burroughs & Mountford, of Trenton, New Jersey, operated from 1879 to the late 1800s and produced some highly decorative wares, including Flow Blue.

This mark was used between 1879 and 1895.

Plate (8") with scalloped edge and fluting. Features a bouquet of chrysanthemums on a pink and white background, gold highlights on the rim.
$35.00 – 45.00.

Carrollton Pottery Company

This company operated as the Carrollton Pottery Co. from 1903 to the 1930s, in Carrollton, Ohio. Though the quality of its products varied over the years, it produced many good quality decorative pieces.

Advertising plate (8¼") with roses.
$35.00 – 45.00.

This mark was used from about 1903 to about 1910.

Plate (8¾") with violets. $30.00 – 40.00.

Platter (13" x 9¼") with grapes.
$60.00 – 75.00.

Portrait plate (9¼"). $40.00 – 50.00.

Figural plate (10").
$55.00 – 65.00.

Bowl (10¼") with plums. $10.00 – 20.00.

Flow Blue platter (14" x 10") with fruit.
$135.00 – 155.00.

Cartwright Brothers

The Cartwright Brothers began operations as the Cartwright Bros. Co. in 1896 in East Liverpool, Ohio, and operated until about 1924. Today, the wares of this company are not commonly found.

No reference was found for this mark, but I would place it in the latter years of the company. Reads "GLENDORA."

Platter (13" x 10") with fruit and green lustre border. $45.00 – 55.00.

Chesapeake Pottery

Chesapeake Pottery of Baltimore, Maryland, began in 1880, and in 1882 became D.F. Haynes & Co. Several name variations followed, and the company closed in 1914. It produced fine wares. The following mark is one commonly found.

This mark was used from about 1900 to about 1914.

Pitcher (6½″) with floral design.
$65.00 – 75.00. From the collection of Faye Lyon.

Jardinière (7½″) with water lilies. $125.00 – 150.00.
From the collection of Faye Lyon.

Jardinière (5½″) with lion ornaments.
$75.00 – 85.00.

Colonial Pottery Company

The Colonial Pottery Company operated in East Liverpool, Ohio, from 1903 to 1929.

This mark was used from about 1903 to about 1915.

Advertising plate (9¾") with portrait.
$40.00 – 50.00.

Mug (5") with artist. $35.00 – 45.00.

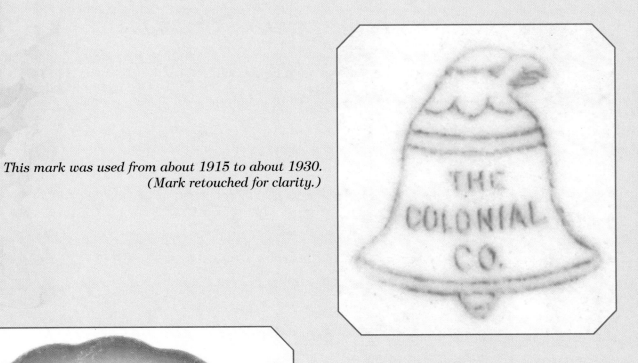

This mark was used from about 1915 to about 1930. (Mark retouched for clarity.)

Platter (12½″ x 9¾″) with flowers and pink border. $35.00 – 45.00.

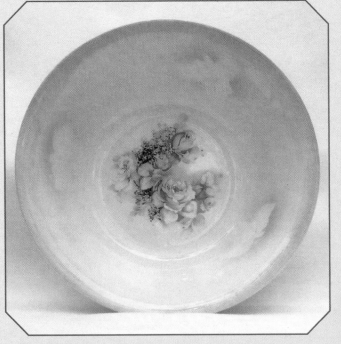

Bowl (9¾″) with flowers and pink lustre $20.00 – 30.00.

Tankard (13") with grapes. $135.00 – 155.00.

Mug (4½"), which would have matched a pitcher or tankard. $35.00 – 45.00.

Mug (4½"), which was part of a lemonade set. $25.00 – 35.00.

Columbian Art Pottery Company

Established by W.T. Morris and F.R. Willmore, this company was in operation from 1893 to about 1902, in Trenton, New Jersey, and produced specialty pieces in porcelain and whiteware. These wares are a bit difficult to find.

This mark was used from 1893 to 1902.

Mug (5″) with figural scene. $35.00 – 45.00.

Mug (5″) with monk. $35.00 – 45.00.

Plate (6¾″) with flowers. $20.00 – 30.00.

Plate (7″) with gold trim. $20.00 – 30.00.

Plate (6¾″) with flowers. $20.00 – 30.00.

A variation of the previous mark. Reads "COLUMBIAN ART CHINA."

Plate (6¾″) with flowers. $20.00 – 30.00.

Cook Pottery Company

The Cook Pottery Co. operated from 1894 to the 1920s, in Trenton, New Jersey.

This mark was used from about 1900 to about 1910. Reads "ETRURIA MELLOR & CO."

Plate (8¼") with fruit. $35.00 – 45.00.

Plate (11½") with flowers. $35.00 – 45.00.

1910 calendar plate (8¼") with flowers. $45.00 – 55.00.

Crescent China Company

The Crescent China Co., of Alliance, Ohio, began around 1920 and operated until about 1927, when it became Leigh Potters, Inc. Because the Crescent China Co. was owned by members of the Sebring family, you will often see almost identical wares from the two companies. (See Limoges China and French China for similar pieces.)

This mark was used about 1924. (The "24" in mark likely indicates 1924.)

Advertising plate (9¼") with wildlife scene. $25.00 – 35.00.

Game platter (11¾" x 9") with pheasant. Decal incorporates artist's signature, Daudin. $45.00 – 55.00.

Game plate (7") with snipe. Decal incorporates artist's signature, Daudin. $15.00 – 25.00.

Game plate (7") with pheasant. Decal incorporates artist's signature, Daudin. $15.00 – 25.00.

Close-up of Daudin signature on decal.

This mark is a mystery. Some authors have attributed it to the Crescent China Company of Alliance, Ohio, while others suggest it may be an earlier mark, perhaps of the Warner-Keffer China Co. It may also have been a decorating company, which could explain the second mark below. For reference, I have listed it under the name incorporated in the mark.

Dates of this mark are unknown, but DeBolt reports to have found it on a plate dated 1912.

*Bowl (10¾") with roses and green lustre border.
$35.00 – 45.00.*

These marks may indicate that Crescent China acquired stock from Dresden China to supplement its own, or that it simply decorated wares rather than produced them.

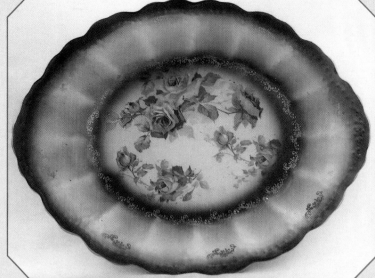

Bowl (10¾") with beaded border. $35.00 – 45.00.

Platter (15"x11¾") with roses and green border, marked "Crescent China K" and "Dresden Porcelain." $65.00 – 75.00. *From the collection of Faye Lyon.*

Crooksville China Company

This company had a long history in the American pottery industry. It was in operation for over 50 years, from 1902 to 1959, in Crooksville, Ohio.

This mark was used from about 1907 to about 1920. Reads "STERLING PORCELAIN." (Mark retouched for clarity.)

Advertising plate (6¼") with fruit. $25.00 – 35.00.

Bowl (10¼″) with fruit. $20.00 – 30.00.

Plate (10¼″) with roses. $35.00 – 45.00.
Marked "STINTHAL CHINA" (see below).

This mark was used from about 1910 to about
1920. Reads "STINTHAL CHINA."

Footed bowl (8¾" across, 5" high) with flowers. $75.00 – 85.00.

Pitcher (7") with fruit. $60.00 – 70.00.

Dresden Pottery

Dresden Pottery operated from 1876 to about 1927, during which time it used several different names. From 1876 to about 1882, it was Brunt, Bloor, Martin & Co. From 1882 to around 1915, it was the Potters' Cooperative Co., and from about 1916 to about 1925, it used T. P. C. O. Co. From 1890 to 1915 it usually used the name DRESDEN in its mark, and did so again from around 1925 to around 1927. Many of its decorative pieces found on the market today are marked with a wreath and the word DRESDEN and date prior to 1915. The DRESDEN name is sometimes confused with the German Dresden porcelain, but the wares are quite different. Dresden produced whiteware and semi-porcelain, in contrast to the German porcelain company. Dresden pieces are plentiful and often feature fruit or animals, such as deer decals designed by R.K. Beck.

This mark was used in about the 1890s.

Plate (9½") with embossing. $35.00 – 45.00.

Plate (9") with embossed napkin pattern. $55.00 – 65.00.

Plate (7½") with embossing.
$30.00 – 40.00.

This mark was used in about the 1890s.

Dish (13½"x7") with handles.
$50.00 – 60.00.

This mark, used from about 1900, has been attributed to Dresden Pottery, though some question this association because it is unlike Dresden's other marks. Reads "PERFECT."

Large plate (12") with cobalt border.
$75.00 – 85.00.

This mark was used from about 1895 to about 1905.

Platter (11¾"x8½") with fruit. $45.00 – 55.00.

Plate (9") with snipe. $20.00 – 30.00.

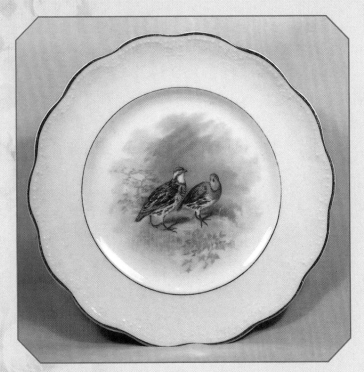

This mark was used from about 1905 to about 1910.

Plate (7″) with birds. $20.00 – 30.00.

Plate (7¾″) with fruit. $25.00 – 35.00.

Plate (10½") with country scene, which was part of a series of the four seasons. Front reads "Summer." $35.00 – 45.00.

Plate (10") with portrait. $35.00 – 45.00.

Plate (10") with cherries. $35.00 – 45.00.

Platter (11¼"x 9") with roses. $55.00 – 65.00.

This mark was used from about 1908 to about 1915.

Plate (10½") with grapes. Decal incorporates artist's signature, Daudin. $40.00 – 50.00.

Plate (10½") with fruit. $35.00 – 45.00.

Plate (9¼") with fruit. $35.00 – 45.00.

Plate (9¼") with roses. $35.00 – 45.00.

Plate (10") with flowers. $30.00 – 40.00.

Plate (8½") with flowers. $35.00 – 45.00.

Plate (9½") with roses. $35.00 – 45.00.

Plate (9¼") with fruit. $35.00 – 45.00.

Plate (10½") with fruit. $35.00 – 45.00.

Plate (10¼") with flowers. $35.00 – 45.00.

Plate (9¼") with roses. $35.00 – 45.00.

Plate (6½") with fruit. $15.00 – 25.00.

Advertising plate (6½") from Christy series.
$30.00 – 40.00.

Advertising plate (6½") from Christy series.
$30.00 – 40.00.

Plate (7½") with Dutch scene.
$25.00 – 35.00.

1911 Calendar plate (8½") featuring
times around the world. $65.00 – 75.00.

Large plate (13") with wildlife scene. Decal incorporates artist's signature, R. K. Beck. $55.00 – 65.00.

Souvenir plate (7½") with bathing beauty. $35.00 – 45.00.

Bowl (10¼") with roses. $20.00 – 30.00.

Bowl (10") with roses. $20.00 – 30.00.

Bowl (9½") with roses. $20.00 – 30.00.

Plate (8") with roses. $35.00 – 45.00.

Plate (10½″) with portrait. $75.00 – 85.00.

Pitcher (8″) with roses. $55.00 – 65.00.

Lemonade pitcher (5¾″) with fruit. $75.00 – 85.00.

Cups (4½") with fruit, made to accompany a lemonade pitcher.
$25.00 – 35.00 each.

Cups (4½") with fruit, made to accompany a lemonade
pitcher. $25.00 – 35.00 each.

Lemonade pitcher (5¾") with fruit.
$75.00 – 85.00.

Lemonade pitcher (5¾") with flowers. Decal incorporates artist's signature, Aliec. $75.00 – 85.00.

Cup (4½") with fruit, made to accompany a lemonade pitcher. $25.00 – 35.00 each.

Close up of signature on decal.

Cup (4½") with flowers, made to accompany a lemonade pitcher. $25.00 – 35.00.

*Cup (4½″) with fruit, made to accompany a
lemonade pitcher. $25.00 – 35.00.*

*Mug (4¼″) with Dutch theme.
$25.00 – 35.00.*

Backside of mug.

This mark was used from about 1920 to about 1925. Reads "T. P. C. O. Co. SEMI-VIT." "20" indicates the year 1920.

Lemonade pitcher (6¾") with flowers. Decal incorporates artist's signature, Gorno. $75.00 – 85.00.

Close up of signature on decal.

This mark was used from about 1920 to about 1925. Reads "THE POTTER'S CO-OPERATIVE."

Lemonade pitcher (6½") with roses.
$75.00 – 85.00.

East End China Company

In about 1909, the East End Pottery Co. of East Liverpool, Ohio, used the name East End China Co. Shortly thereafter, it was taken over by the Trenle China Co.

This mark was used from about 1909 to about 1910. Reads "E. E. C. CO."

Advertising plate (8") with windmill.
$35.00 – 45.00.

Plate (10¼") with deer. Decal incorporates artist's signature, R. K. Beck. $45.00 – 55.00.

Plate (9") with dog portrait. $45.00 – 55.00.

Plate (10¼") with grapes and luster border. $35.00 – 45.00.

East Liverpool Potteries Company

In 1900, six potteries banded together and formed the East Liverpool Potteries Co. in East Liverpool, Ohio. Four of the companies dropped out in 1903, and the remaining two did so in 1907.

This mark was used from about 1900 to about 1907.

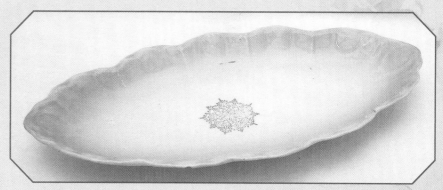

Dish (12¾" x 6½") with green border. $20.00 – 30.00.

Plate (9") with birds. $35.00 – 45.00.

Bowl (6") with waterfall. $15.00 – 25.00.

East Liverpool Pottery Company

The East Liverpool Pottery Company operated in East Liverpool, Ohio, from 1894 to 1900.

This mark was used during the company's brief six year operation from 1894 to about 1900. Reads "E. L. P. Co."

Pitcher (8") with portrait. $125.00 – 150.00.

Mug (5") with Dutch theme. $35.00 – 45.00. Note the same decal used by Dresden, p. 65.

This mark is a variation of the previous mark. Reads "NARCISSUS."

Dish (11½"x 6") with flowers. $25.00 – 35.00.

East Palestine Pottery Company

The East Palestine Pottery Company operated in East Palestine, Ohio, from 1884 to 1909 when its name was changed to the W.S. George Pottery Co.

This mark was used from about 1900. Reads "The E. P .P. CO." (Mark retouched for clarity.)

Plate (9") with country scene. $35.00 – 45.00.

This mark was used from about 1905 to about 1909.
Reads "IRIS E. P. P. CO." (Mark retouched for clarity.)

Plate (11¼") with portrait of Queen Louise of
Prussia, a popular subject for portrait
plates of this era. $75.00 – 85.00.

Empire Pottery

Empire Pottery, of Trenton, New Jersey, was in operation from about 1880 to 1892.

This mark was used from 1885 to about 1890.

Plate (9") with a Moss Rose pattern,
popular during this period.
This is an example of stoneware.
$40.00 – 50.00.

Ford China Company

The Ford China Co., of Ford City, Pennsylvania, operated from about 1889 to about 1910.

*This mark was used from about 1900.
The monogram in the center is "F. C. Co."
(Mark retouched for clarity.)*

Plate (9¼") with flowers. $35.00 – 45.00.

French China Company

The French China Company started in 1898 in East Liverpool, Ohio, and within a few years moved to Sebring, Ohio, where it operated until about 1929.

*This mark was used before 1905. Reads
"La Francaise Porcelain."*

*Plate (11") with thistles.
$55.00 – 65.00.*

Dish (13¾" x 10¾") with violets and green border. $55.00 – 65.00.

Dish (13¾" x 10¾") with violets and pale pink border. $55.00 – 65.00.

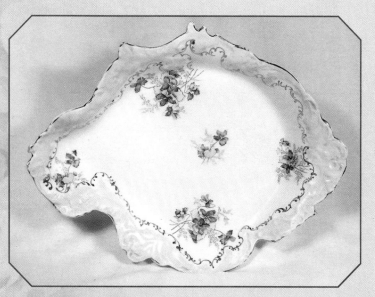

Dish (13¾" x 10¾") with violets and yellow border. $55.00 – 65.00.

Dish (13¾" x 11") with flowers and embossed shell accents.
$85.00 – 95.00.

This mark was used from about 1905 to about 1915. It is a common mark and is often found on Flow Blue.

Plate (7¾") with fruit and Flow Blue border.
$25.00 – 35.00.

Plate (7¾") with fruit and Flow Blue border.
$25.00 – 35.00.

Plate (9") with birds. $20.00 – 30.00.

Plate (9") with birds. $20.00 – 30.00.

Bowl (9½") with orange lustre border.
$25.00 – 35.00.

Bowl (9½") with green lustre border.
$25.00 – 35.00.

Fish platter (13¼"x 10") with blue background. $75.00 – 85.00.

Dish (14"x 8") with purple border. $45.00 – 55.00.

Dish (12¾" x 9½") with flowers. $45.00 – 55.00.

Plate (7¼") with roses. $25.00 – 35.00.

Plate (8½") with portrait. $35.00 – 45.00.

Bowl (9½") with fruit. $25.00 – 35.00.

Plate (8¼") with fruit. $20.00 – 30.00.

Plate (8¼") with fruit. $20.00 – 30.00.

Dish (6"x 4") with roses. $15.00 – 25.00.

Platter (13½" x 10") with ducks. $75.00 – 85.00.

Platter (13½"x 10") with pheasant.
$75.00 – 85.00.

Game plate (8½"). $20.00 – 30.00.

Game plate (8½"). $20.00 – 30.00.

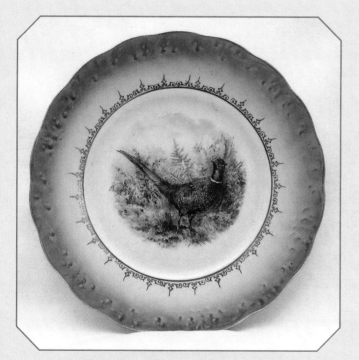

Game plate (8½"). $20.00 – 30.00.

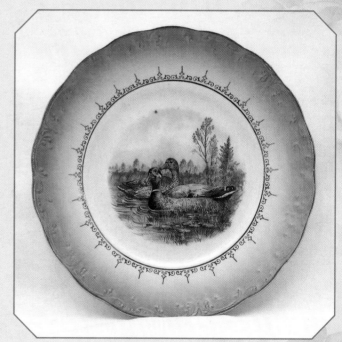

Game plate (8½"). $20.00 – 30.00.

Game plate (8½"). $20.00 – 30.00.　　　*Game plate (8½"). $20.00 – 30.00.*

Mugs (4½"). $25.00 – 35.00 each.

This mark was used from about 1905 to about 1915. Reads "LA FRANCAISE SEMI VITREOUS."

Plate (9½") with Flow Blue border. $40.00 – 50.00.

Bowl (8½") with Flow Blue border. $40.00 – 50.00.

Bowl (8½") with teal border. $30.00 – 40.00.

Pitcher (6¾″) with teal border. $55.00 – 65.00.

Platter (13″ x 10″) with Flow Blue border.
$135.00 – 155.00.

This mark was used from about 1918. The "18" in the mark indicates the year, 1918. Reads "F. C. CO."

Platter (13½" x 10¾") with pheasant.
$45.00 – 55.00.

W.S. George Pottery

The W.S. George Pottery started in 1909, in East Palestine, Ohio, when William Shaw George changed the name of the East Palestine Pottery Co. to W.S. George Pottery. The company operated until the late 1950s.

This mark was used before 1920.

Plate (9") with fish, most likely part of a fish set.
$20.00 – 30.00.

Globe Pottery Company

The Globe Pottery Co. operated under this name from 1888 to 1900, and again from 1907 to 1912. From 1901 to 1907, it was a part of a group of companies operating under the name East Liverpool Potteries Co.

This mark was used from about 1890 to about 1900.

Calendar plate (7¼"), 1910, with advertising.
$45.00 – 55.00.

Plate (9¼") with flowers. $25.00 – 35.00.

Plate (8″) with fruit. $25.00 – 35.00.

Plate (8¼″) with flowers. $25.00 – 35.00.

Plate (6½″) with portrait of Queen Louise of Prussia.
$25.00 – 35.00.

Plate (6¼") with American history theme. Reads "LANDING OF THE PILGRIMS." $20.00 – 30.00.

Plate (6¼") with American history theme. Reads "LANDING OF COLUMBUS." $20.00 – 30.00.

Goodwin Pottery Company

The Goodwin Pottery Co. of East Liverpool, Ohio, operated from 1893 to 1912. The Goodwin family had been producing pottery as early as 1844, which explains the date on the following two marks. The Goodwin Pottery Company (according to *DeBolt's*) also produced a very decorative line called Usona. The Usona line features items very similar to the popular Warwick Ioga line. Since Usona is not as well known as Ioga, it represents an excellent value for the collector at the present time. This is sure to change, however, as more collectors discover Usona. Usona pieces are less common, and even reference photos are hard to come by, so I have included numerous pieces even though some are priced above the general range of this collection.

This mark was used from 1893 to about 1904.

Plate (9¼") with advertising on back.
$45.00 – 55.00.

This mark is a slight variation
of the previous mark, dropping
"THE" from the name.

Plate (10") with flowers. $30.00 – 40.00.

Plate (8½") with flowers. $25.00 – 35.00.

Plate (8½") with flowers. $25.00 – 35.00.

Plate (10") with flowers. $30.00 – 40.00.

Lemonade pitcher (6¼") with exotic bird. Matte finish.
$75.00 – 85.00.

*This mark was used from about 1905 to about 1912
(according to DeBolt's). Note: Because of the similarities between Usona and Warwick Ioga pieces, collectors may find that some of their unmarked
Warwick pieces may actually be unmarked Usona.*

Lemonade pitcher (6¼") with fruit. Reads "LEMONADE
JUG" on base, in red. $75.00 – 85.00.

Cup (4½") with exotic bird, made to accompany a
lemonade pitcher. Matte finish. $25.00 – 35.00.

Lemonade pitcher (6") with fruit. $80.00 – 90.00.

Cup (4½"), probably part of a lemon-ade set. $25.00 – 35.00.

Nut bowl (6" wide x 10" across) with flowers. Reads "NUT BOWL" on inside of bowl, in red. $75.00 – 95.00.

Vase (11¼″) with flowers.
$140.00 – 150.00.

Vase (8½″) with roses.
$125.00 – 135.00.

Vase (10½″) with berries. Reads
"PRINCE VASE" on base, in red.
$125.00 – 150.00.

Vase (10½″) with flowers. Reads "No. 1 BOUQUET VASE" on base, in red. $125.00 – 150.00.

Vase (10½″) with flowers. Reads "No.1 BOUQUET VASE" on base, in red. $125.00 – 150.00.

Vase (10½″) with flowers. Reads "VASSAR VASE" on base, in red. $125.00 – 150.00.

Vase (3¼") with monk. Reads "NASTURTIUM VASE" on base, in red. $85.00 – 95.00.

Mug (5") with portrait. $55.00 – 65.00.

Mug (5") with portrait. $55.00 – 65.00.

Mug (5") with portrait. $55.00 – 65.00.

*Vase (11¾″) with portrait.
Reads "No. 3 VASE" on base,
in red. $160.00 – 180.00.*

*Vase (12¼″) with flowers. Matte
finish. $125.00 – 145.00.*

*Vase (15″) with portrait.
$155.00 – 175.00.*

Tankard (13¼″) with monk.
$155.00 – 175.00.

Tankard (13¼″) with portrait. Decal incorpo-
rates artist's signature, G. Bonfits.
$175.00 – 195.00.

Close up of signature on decal.

Tankard (13¼") with portrait. Decal incorporates artist's signature, G. Bonfits.
$175.00 – 195.00.

Vase (10") with portrait. Decal incorporates artist's signature, G. Bonfits.
$175.00 – 195.00.

Vase (10") with figural scene. Reads "TIFFANY VASE" on base, in red. $225.00 – 250.00.

This mark is similar to the Usona mark and used around the same period, from about 1905 to 1912.

Pitcher (7") with flowers. $55.00 – 65.00.

Harker Pottery Company

Benjamin Harker, Sr., began making pottery in 1840. In 1889, the Harker Pottery Co. name was incorporated in East Liverpool, Ohio, and the company remained in business as such until 1972. Later Harker pieces from the 1930s and 1940s are widely collected today.

This mark was used from 1890 to about 1920.

Platter (10¾" x 8") with buck and brown embossed rim.
$45.00 – 55.00.

Plate (10") with yellow lustre, embossed border, and fruit. $40.00 – 50.00.

Souvenir plate (9¼") with buck and green accent.
Reads "SOUVENIR OGDENSBURG, N.Y."
$35.00 – 45.00.

Advertising plate (7¼") with religious theme.
$15.00 – 25.00.

Advertising plate (9") with roses. $35.00 – 45.00.

Advertising plate (8¾"), shows boy looking at sign
(where advertisment would have been). Reads
"THAT'S WHERE WE'LL GO."
$35.00 – 45.00.

Plate (9¾") with schoolhouse. Reads "THE LITTLE
RED SCHOOLHOUSE." $35.00 – 45.00.

Plate (6½") with country scene. Reads "Summer."
$20.00 – 30.00.

Imperial China

I have listed the two marks in this section under Imperial China because their maker has not been established, but it may have been the Ohio China Co. Note the similarities between the two marks. Though they appear identical, the second mark has a slightly different bent, which I call a backstroke.

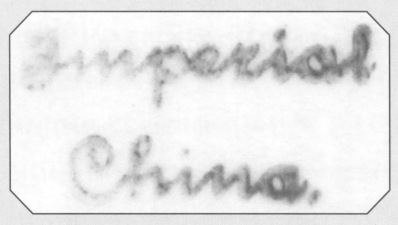

This mark was most likely used around 1900.

Plate (9″) with roses. $35.00 – 45.00.

Plate (9″) with roses. $35.00 – 45.00.

Calendar plate (8¼″) with western theme, 1911. $55.00 – 65.00.

Plate (9¼″) with wildlife. $25.00 – 35.00.

Plate (6″) with portrait, part of a series featuring first ladies. Reads "MARTHA WASHINGTON."
$25.00 – 35.00.

This backstroke mark was most likely used around 1900. Notice the fancy C and the elongated and backward stroke on the P.

Plate (9″) with boats. $25.00 – 35.00.

Plate (6″) with portrait, part of a series featuring first ladies. Reads "MRS. ROOSEVELT."
$25.00 – 35.00.

Plate (7¼″) with roses. $30.00 – 40.00.

Plate (8½″) with Flow Blue. $55.00 – 65.00.

International Pottery Company

The International Pottery Co. of Trenton, New Jersey, was in business from 1860 to about 1930. During its long life, this company used many names and a variety of marks.

This mark was used from about 1903 to about 1910. Reads "ROYAL CHINA BURGESS & CO."

Plate (8¼") with monk. $35.00 – 45.00.

Plate (8¼") with roses. $25.00 – 35.00.

Bowl (10") with roses. $20.00 – 30.00.

Edwin M. Knowles Company

This company operated from 1901 to 1963, in East Liverpool, Ohio, though its factory was located in Chester, West Virginia, with another plant (added in 1913) in Newell, West Virginia. It was one of the largest producers of dinnerware of the period and produced good quality wares.

This mark (with no numbers) was used from 1901 to 1909.

Plate (8") with cherries. $30.00 – 40.00.

Plate (8") with boats. $30.00 – 40.00.

Plate (8") with strawberries. $30.00 – 40.00.

Plate (8¼") with advertising. $30.00 – 40.00.

This mark (with three separate numbers) was used from about 1910 to about 1930. The "16" in the mark indicates the year, 1916.

Platter (13½" x 9¾") with fish. $75.00 – 85.00.

Platter (15½" x 11¼") with fish. $75.00 – 85.00.

Knowles, Taylor & Knowles Company

There are many books on the Knowles, Taylor and Knowles Company of East Liverpool, Ohio, which operated from 1854 to 1929. The company's history is well known, and its wares widely sought after. (Of special interest is its Lotus Ware line of museum-quality porcelain, produced in the 1890s.) The Knowles, Taylor and Knowles eagle mark is very recognizable and was used in various forms from around 1880 to around 1900. They produced commemorative as well as decorative china, including pieces for Masonic conventions. KTK is a delight to collect, because the company made such a variety of good quality wares.

This mark was used from about 1890 to about 1907.

Commemorative plate (8") with cherubs.
$55.00 – 65.00.

Commemorative plate (8") with cobalt border.
$65.00 – 75.00.

Commemorative plate (8") with ducks.
$55.00 – 65.00.

Commemorative plate (8″) with ducks.
$55.00 – 65.00.

Commemorative plate (8″) with cobalt border.
$75.00 – 85.00.

Commemorative plate (8″) with couple.
$65.00 – 75.00.

Portrait plate (8") featuring Marechal Lefebure.
$75.00 – 85.00.

Portrait plate (8") with Admiral Dewey.
$85.00 – 95.00.

Commemorative plate (8") with shepard.
$55.00 – 65.00.

Back of preceding plate.

Commemorative plate (8") with Columbus.
$55.00 – 65.00.

Back of preceding plate.

Commemorative plate (8") with couple.
$65.00 – 75.00.

Back of preceding plate.

Commemorative plate (8") with family.
$65.00 – 75.00.

Back of preceding plate.

This mark was used from about
1900 to 1915.

Jardinière (8½" high x 9¼"across).
$65.00 – 75.00.

Jardinière(7" high x 8"across). $125.00 – 150.00.

Pitcher (8") with flowers. $55.00 – 65.00.

Plate (10¼") with roses. $45.00 – 55.00.

Plate (10½") with roses. Decal incorporates artist's signature, Guyeau. $35.00 – 45.00

Plate (9¼") with waterfall. Decal incorporates artist's signature. $45.00 – 55.00.

Close up of signature on decal.

Plate (9½") with roses. $35.00 – 45.00.

Plate (10") with roses. $35.00 – 45.00.

Plate (9¼") with woman and child. $45.00 – 55.00.

Plate (9¼") with Martha Washington.
$35.00 – 45.00.

Plate (9¼") with George Washington.
$35.00 – 45.00.

Plate (9¼") with water wheel. Reads "Laney Wheel
IOM." $35.00 – 45.00.

*Calendar plate (10") with advertising, 1911. Mark
includes "302." $45.00 – 55.00.*

Plate (9¼") with Crusader theme, $65.00 – 75.00.

Plate (9¼") with Crusader theme. $65.00 – 75.00.

Plate (9¼″) with Crusader theme. $65.00 – 75.00.

Plate (9¼″) with Crusader theme. $65.00 – 75.00.

This mark was probably used about 1900.

Advertising plate (7") with portrait. $45.00 – 55.00.

This mark was used from about 1907 to about 1915. Reads "K. T. &K. CO. RAMONA."

Game plate (9¼") with fish. $25.00 – 35.00.

Game plate (9¼″) with birds. $25.00 – 35.00.

Game plate (9¼″) with birds. $25.00 – 35.00.

Platter (13½″x10″) with turkeys. $75.00 – 85.00.

Game plate (10"). $20.00 – 30.00.

Game plate (10"). $20.00 – 30.00.

Game plate (10"). $20.00 – 30.00.

Game plate (10″). $20.00 – 30.00.

Game plate (10″). $20.00 – 30.00.

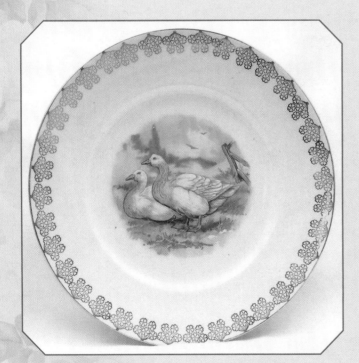

Game plate (10″). $20.00 – 30.00.

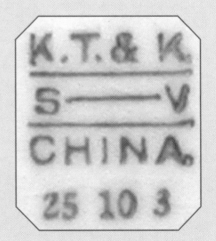

This mark was used from 1905 to 1926. Reads "K. T. & K."

Commemorative plate (8") with portrait of Masonic leader. Reads "MacArthur Grand Master 1913 1914." $50.00 – 60.00.

Back of preceding plate.

Presentation box of preceding plate.

Plate (9″) with ship. $20.00 – 30.00.

This mark was used about the late 1920s.
Reads "K. T. & K. IVORY."

Advertising plate (10″) with ship. $25.00 – 35.00.

Homer Laughlin China Company

Homer Laughlin (pronounced LOCK lin, according to David Conley, Director of Retail Sales & Marketing for the company) began in 1871, in East Liverpool, Ohio, as the Laughlin Brothers Pottery, and in 1907 moved across the Ohio River to Newell, West Virginia, where it is still in operation today, producing the popular Fiesta® dinnerware pattern. The company estimates it has produced 25,000 china patterns in its long history. Of special interest is its Laughlin Art China line, which is widely collected and brings premium prices. There are numerous books on the market featuring many of Homer Laughlin's most popular patterns and early wares.

This mark was used from about 1897 to about 1905. It may read "AN AMERICAN BEAUTY," "GOLDEN GATE," or "COLONIAL."

Plate (6½") with fruit. $25.00 – 35.00.

This mark was used from about 1900. It may read "COLONIAL."

This mark was used from about 1905.

Plate (10") with flowers. $45.00 – 55.00.

Plate (9¼") with currants, a popular decoration for Laughlin Art China. The currant theme included a variety of berries, including gooseberries, grapes, and others. $75.00 – 95.00.

Large plate (12") with currants. $95.00 – 115.00.

This mark was used from 1903 to about 1920.

Tankard (12¼″) with monk.
$175.00 – 195.00.

Plate (10″) with flowers. $25.00 – 35.00.

Calendar plate (8") dated 1909. $55.00 – 65.00.

Souvenir bowl (6") with sailboats. $15.00 – 25.00.

Bowl (7") with sunset. $15.00 – 25.00.

Advertising plate (9") with currants.
$35.00 – 45.00.

This mark is a variation of the preceding mark and was used from about 1908 to about 1915. Reads "HOMER LAUGHLIN The Angelus."

Platter (17"x12½") with fish.
$75.00 – 85.00.

This mark, with a letter, single digit number, and letter was used from 1922 to 1929. The first letter indicates the month (A=Jan., L=Dec.,), the number indicates the year (5=1925), and the last letter indicates the plant where produced (N=factory N).

Bowl (10") with roses. Mark includes "L 5 N."
$20.00 – 30.00.

Advertising plate (9¾") with horseshoe. Mark
includes "K 7 N." $35.00 – 45.00.

Platter (8½" x 6") with bird. Mark includes "H 7 N5." $20.00 – 30.00.

This mark for Lebeau Porcelaine is still a mystery, but most authors agree it belongs somewhere in the Sebring family of potteries. Some believe it was used by Saxon China. I have seen several examples of the Lebeau Porcelaine mark on items also marked with Sebring Pottery marks.

This mark, "Sebring Pottery Specialties," was found on a plate also marked "Lebeau Porcelaine" (plate not pictured).

This mark, "Art Ware, Sebring Pottery Co., Sebring, Ohio," has also been found on items marked "Lebeau Porcelaine." Did Sebring acquire Lebeau stock to decorate, or the reverse? The mystery continues. For now, I have listed it under Lebeau Porcelaine for reference. I suspect the Lebeau Porcelaine mark could have been used from about 1900 to about 1920.

Plate (9") with Dutch scene. $35.00 – 45.00. Marked "Lebeau Porcelain" and "Art Ware Sebring Pottery Co., Sebring Ohio."

Souvenir plate (9") with the words from a popular song first published in 1905, "Everybody works but Father." $35.00 – 45.00.

Mug (5") with monk. $35.00 – 45.00.

Limoges China Company

The Limoges China Company of Sebring, Ohio, was started by Frank Sebring around 1900 (dates vary) and was briefly called Sterling China, then the Sebring China Company. This caused confusion with another Sebring China company, so the name was changed again, this time to Limoges China Co. In the 1940s, it was threatened with legal action by Limoges of France, and the name was changed to the American Limoges China Company. The company closed in the late 1950s.

This mark was used from about 1900 to about 1910.

Game platter (15½"x11¾") with fish. $65.00 – 75.00.

Plate (9½") with fish. $20.00 – 30.00.

Plate (9½") with fish. $20.00 – 30.00.

Plate (9½") with fish. $20.00 – 30.00.

Plate (9") with birds. $20.00 – 30.00.

Plate (9") with birds. $20.00 – 30.00.

Plate (9") with birds. $20.00 – 30.00.

Plate (9") with birds. $20.00 – 30.00.

Plate (9") with birds. $20.00 – 30.00.

Plate (9") with birds. $20.00 – 30.00.

Plate (7") with flowers. $20.00 – 30.00.

Plate (10") with country scene. $25.00 – 35.00.

Plate (10") with flowers. $35.00 – 45.00.

Plate (7") with birds. $20.00 – 30.00.

Plate (7½") with fruit . $20.00 – 30.00.

Bowl (9") with fruit. $25.00 – 35.00.

Bowl (10") with Dutch scene and Flow Blue border. $30.00 – 40.00.

Bowl (9¾") with portrait. $30.00 – 40.00.

Bowl (9¾") with portrait. $30.00 – 40.00.

Bowl (9¾") with fruit. $25.00 – 35.00.

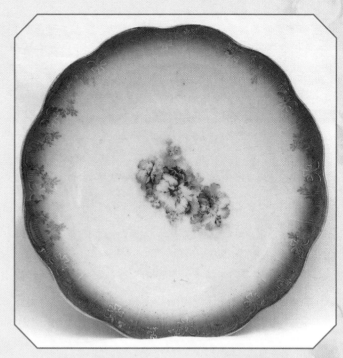

Plate (6¼") with flowers. $15.00 – 25.00.

Plate (8¼") with fish. $20.00 – 30.00.

Plate (9¼") with roses. $35.00 – 45.00.

Plate (9¼") with roses and advertising on back.
$35.00 – 45.00.

Plate (9¼") with roses. $35.00 – 45.00.

Plate (9¼") with flowers and Flow Blue border.
$45.00 – 55.00.

Plate (10") with roses. $45.00 – 55.00.

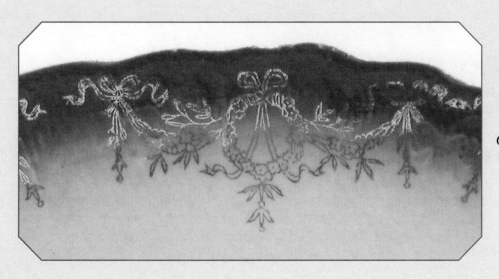

Close up of gold pattern on rim.

Close up of gold pattern on rim.

Close up of gold pattern on rim.

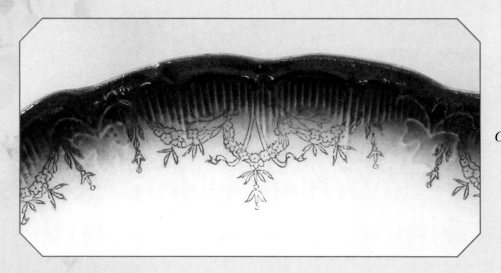

Close up of gold pattern on rim.

Close up of gold pattern on rim.

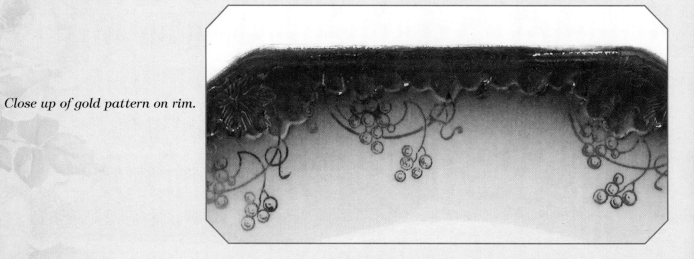

Close up of gold pattern on rim.

Pitcher (7¾") with country scene. $55.00 – 65.00.

Pitcher (10") with Dutch scene. $125.00 – 135.00.

Pitcher (10") with flowers. $125.00 – 135.00.

Pitcher (8¾") with flowers and ice lip.
$115.00 – 125.00.

This mark was used from about 1910 to about 1915.
It is almost identical to the preceding mark.

Plate (8¼") with birds. Decal incorporates artist's
signature, R. K. Beck. $20.00 – 30.00.

Plate (10¼") with flowers and Flow Blue border.
$45.00 – 55.00.

This mark was used in the 1920s. The "24" in the mark indicates the year, 1924.

Plate (9¼") with roses. $25.00 – 35.00.

Plate (8¼") with fruit. Decal incorporates artist's signature. $25.00 – 35.00.

Signature on preceding plate.

Plate (7") with birds. Decal incorporates artist's signature, Daudin. $15.00 – 25.00.

Plate (7") with birds. Decal incorporates artist's signature, Daudin. $15.00 – 25.00.

Plate (7") with birds. Decal incorporates artist's signature, Daudin. $15.00 – 25.00.

Plate (7") with birds. Decal incorporates artist's signature, Daudin. $15.00 – 25.00.

Plate (7") with birds. Decal incorporates artist's signature, Daudin. $15.00 – 25.00.

Plate (7") with birds. Decal incorporates artist's signature, Daudin. $15.00 – 25.00.

Plate (7") with birds. Decal incorporates artist's signature, Daudin. $15.00 – 25.00.

D. E. McNicol Pottery Company

The D.E. McNicol Pottery Company began operating in 1892 in East Liverpool, Ohio. It also operated a factory in Clarksville, West Virginia. It produced average quality whiteware, including many specialty and commemorative pieces that are easy to find. Most commonly found today are its calendar and advertising pieces.

This Carnation McNicol mark was used from about 1900 to about 1920.

Plate (10¼") with flowers. $30.00 – 40.00.

Plate (9") with flowers. $30.00 – 40.00.

Platter (12" x 9½") with fruit. $55.00 – 65.00.

Figural plate (8¼") with advertising.
$30.00 – 40.00.

Plate (8¼") with pansies. $30.00 – 40.00.

Pitcher (6¼″) with roses. $75.00 – 85.00.

Pitcher (6½″) with flowers. $75.00 – 85.00.

This mark was used from about 1905 to about 1915.

Advertising plate (8¼") commemorating the Panama Canal, dated 1915. $55.00 – 65.00.

Plate (10") with roses. $25.00 – 35.00.

Plate (9¼") with wildlife scene. $25.00 – 35.00.

This mark was used from about 1915 to about 1929. May include letters and/or numbers.

Platter (13½" x 10½") with pheasant. $75.00 – 85.00.

Plate (8½") with birds. $20.00 – 30.00.

Calendar plate (9¼") commemorating the signing of the Versailles Treaty and end of WWI. Dated 1919. $45.00 – 55.00.

Advertising plate (9") with unusual harness racing
theme. $55.00 – 65.00.

Plate (10") with roses. $35.00 – 45.00.

Advertising plate (9") with quail. Decal incorporates
artist's signature, Edwin Megargee.
$25.00 – 35.00.

Plate (10″) with fruit. $25.00 – 35.00.

Plate (9″) with flowers. $25.00 – 35.00.

Advertising plate (8¼″) with deer. $25.00 – 35.00.

Advertising plate (8¼") with country scene.
$25.00 – 35.00.

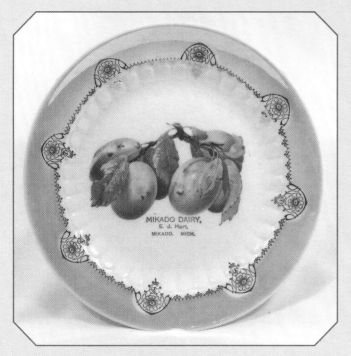

Advertising plate (9") with fruit. $25.00 – 35.00.   *Plate (9¼") with flowers. $25.00 – 35.00.*

*Advertising plate (8¼") commemorating the signing
of the Versailles Treaty on June 28, 1919.
$55.00 – 65.00.*

*Advertising plate (9¼") commemorating the signing
of the cease fire agreement with Germany,
Nov. 11, 1918. $55.00 – 65.00.*

*Advertising plate (9") with birds. Decal incorporates
artist's signature, Edwin Megargee.
$25.00 – 35.00.*

Advertising plate (8½") with fruit. $25.00 – 35.00.

Plate (8") with flowers. $25.00 – 35.00.

Plate (8") with country scene. $20.00 – 30.00.

*Plate (8¼") with pheasant. Decal incorporates
artist's signature, Daudin. $15.00 – 25.00.*

Plate (9¼") with fruit. $20.00 – 30.00.

*Plate (9") with depiction of the Crusades.
$35.00 – 45.00.*

Bowl (10") with fruit. $20.00 – 30.00.

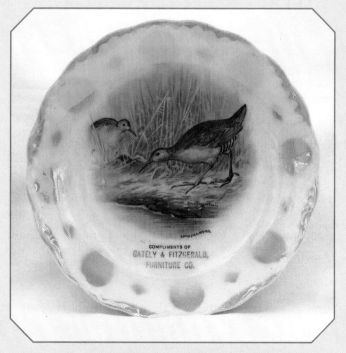

Plate (7¼") with birds. Decal incorporates artist's signature, Edwin Megargee. $25.00 – 35.00.

Plate (7") with birds. Decal incorporates artist's signature, Edwin Megargee. Artist's signature is slightly different from that on preceding plate. $25.00 – 35.00.

McNicol-Smith Company

The McNicol-Smith Company of Wellsville, Ohio, was in operation from 1899 to 1907. The company was formed by D.E. McNicol and William Smith.

This mark was used from 1899 to about 1901. It reads "M&S SEMI PORCELAIN."

Pitcher (10") and cup (3¾") with roses. Pitcher, $125.00 – 145.00. Cup, $25.00 – 35.00.

Mercer Pottery Company

The Mercer Pottery Company began in Trenton, New Jersey, in 1868 and operated until about 1930.

This mark was used in the 1890s.

Plate (10″) with portrait. $35.00 – 45.00.

National China Company

The National China Company began in East Liverpool, Ohio, in 1899 and in 1911 moved to Salineville, Ohio, where it operated until 1931.

This mark was used from 1900 to 1911.

Dish (8½" x 6") with roses. $35.00 – 45.00.

Plate (9¼") featuring the new Pennsylvania capitol, Harrisburg. $30.00 – 40.00.

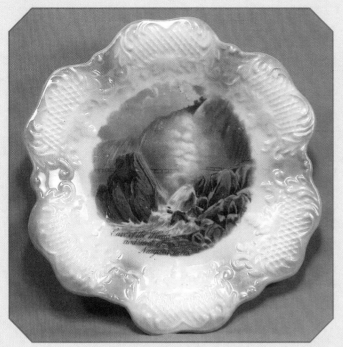

This mark was used from 1900 to 1911. It reads "N. C. Co. E. L. O."

Souvenir plate (7") of Niagra Falls. Decal reads "Cave of the Wings and Rock of Ages Niagra Falls." $35.00 – 45.00.

Plate (9½") with fruit. $40.00 – 50.00.

Plate (9") with berries. $30.00 – 40.00.

Ohio China Company

The Ohio China Company was started in 1896 by the Sebring brothers, in East Palestine, Ohio, and was originally called the Ohio China Works. It was sold and became the Ohio China Company in 1902, and operated until about 1912.

This mark was used from 1896 to about 1902. Reads "O. C. CO. LIMOGES PORCELAIN."

Platter (13¾" x 10½") with ducks. $75.00 – 85.00.

Platter (13¾" x 10½") with birds. $75.00 – 85.00.

Plate (10¼") with portrait of Queen Louise.
$35.00 – 45.00.

Plate (10") with flowers. (Unusual shape.)
$55.00 – 65.00.

Plate (9¼") with roses.
$35.00 – 45.00.

Plate (9¼") with country scene. $30.00 – 40.00.

Dish (12" x 10") with handle. $65.00 – 75.00.

Dish (12" x 10") with handle. $65.00 – 75.00.

Close up of signature on decal.

Advertising plate (9¼") with portrait. Decal incorporates artist's signature, G. Bonfits. $65.00 – 75.00.

Souvenir plate (6¼") with grapes. $20.00 – 30.00.

Tankard (12") with monk. $135.00 – 155.00.

Mug (5") with monk. $45.00 – 55.00.

Mug (5") with monk. $45.00 – 55.00.

Punch bowl (11¼" across x 6" high) with roses.
$150.00 – 175.00.

Pitcher (7½") with roses. $55.00 – 65.00.

Pitcher (5¾") with roses. $65.00 – 75.00.

*This mark was used from about 1902 to about 1912.
Reads "O. C. CO. IMPERIAL CHINA."*

Bowl (10¼") with fruit. $35.00 – 45.00.

Plate (10") with fruit. Back reads "PLAQUE."
$35.00 – 45.00.

Plate (10¼") with roses. Back reads "LARGE CAKE
PLATE No. 19." $35.00 – 45.00.

*Plate (6¼″) with roses. Back reads "SMALL CAKE
PLATE No. 18." $15.00 – 25.00.*

*Bowl (6¼″) with fruit. Back reads "SMALL
BERRY BOWL No. 16." $15.00 – 25.00.*

*Plate (7½″) with Flow Blue border. Back reads "PIE
PLATE 3." $25.00 – 35.00.*

Close up of gold trim.

Plate (8¼") with flowers and Flow Blue border.
Back reads "BREAKFAST PLATE No. 11."
$35.00 – 45.00.

Close up of gold trim.
See the same pattern on Sterling China, p. 232.

174

This mark was used from about 1902 to about 1912. Notice that "O C CO." makes up the mark. Reads "IMPERIAL SEMI VITREOUS CHINA."

Platter (12"x 9½") with watermelon. $100.00 – 125.00.

Plate (7½") with watermelon. $35.00 – 45.00.

Advertising plate (7") with portrait of Queen Louise. $30.00 – 40.00.

Plate (10") with portrait. $45.00 – 55.00.

Plate (9¼") with fruit. $35.00 – 45.00.

Platter (9¾" x 12½") with fish and Flow Blue border.
$135.00 – 155.00.

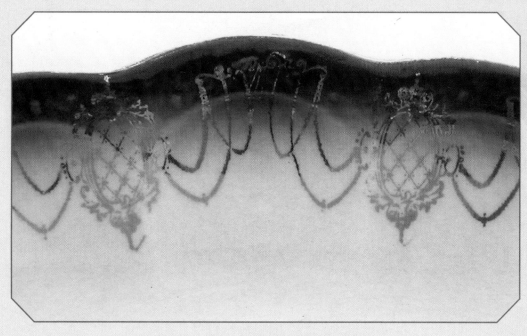

Close up of gold trim.

Oliver China Company

The Oliver China Co. of Sebring, Ohio, operated from 1899 to about 1908. This pottery was another one of the many Sebring Brothers companies.

This mark was used by the Oliver China Co. on the following piece of semi-porcelain, and is an example of how loosely the term "porcelain" was sometimes used. Reads "VERUS PORCE-LAIN." (Mark was retouched for clarity.)

Dish (14½" x 11") with flowers. $65.00 – 75.00.

Onondaga Pottery Company

The Onondaga Pottery Company began in Syracuse, New York, in 1871. In 1966, the name was changed to the Syracuse China Co. In 1995, it was acquired by Libbey, Inc., and is still in business today producing institutional wares.

This mark was used from 1897 to about 1935. A dating system including a number and a letter was commonly used with this mark after 1920. Reads "O. P. Co. SYRACUSE CHINA." (Mark retouched for clarity.)

Plate (9") with monk. (Highly vitrified.) $35.00 – 45.00.

Edward J. Owen China Company

The Edward J. Owen China Co. of Minerva, Ohio, operated from 1902 to about 1930. In 1904, it won a Gold Medal at the St. Louis Exposition and began using "Gold Medal St. Louis" in its mark.

This mark, without a date, was used from about 1905 to about 1915. Reads "GOLD MEDAL ST. LOUIS OWEN MINERVA."

Lemonade pitcher (6") with grapes.
$75.00 – 85.00.

Mug (5") with woman and Foo Dog handle.
$55.00 – 65.00.

*Pitcher (8¼")
with fruit.
$75.00 – 85.00.*

Pitcher (8¼") with grapes. $75.00 – 85.00.

*Tankard (12¼") with portrait.
$125.00 – 150.00.*

Tankard (12¼") with portrait. Same shape as preceding tankard. $125.00 – 150.00.

Mug (5") with portrait. $45.00 – 55.00.

Bowl (7¾") with country scene. $15.00 – 25.00.

Plate (8½") with figural scene. $35.00 – 45.00.

Plate (9¼") with advertising on back. $35.00 – 45.00.

Plate (9¼") with advertising on back. $35.00 – 45.00.

Plate (10½″) with portrait. $40.00 – 50.00.

This mark was used in the 1920s. The "25" in the mark would indicate the year, 1925. Reads "GOLD MEDAL ST. LOUIS OWEN CHINA MINERVA."

Platter (15½″ x 12″) with roses. $45.00 – 55.00.

Platter (13½" x 10½") with country scene. $35.00 – 45.00.

This mark was not found in any reference book, but it would date after 1904 since it uses "GOLD MEDAL" in the mark. (Mark retouched for clarity.)

Platter (12¼" x 9") with cows. $65.00 – 75.00.

Pope – Gosser China Company

The Pope-Gosser China Company was started by Charles F. Gosser and Bentley Pope in Coshocton, Ohio, in 1902. In the company's early years, it experimented with high quality decorative pieces with interesting shapes, and later concentrated on producing dinnerware. The company closed in 1958.

This mark was used from 1903 to about 1908. The Clarus Ware mark is not well known, so it represents a great opportunity for the collector who is lucky enough to find it, because prices are still affordable.

Plate (8¼") with Flow Blue. $55.00 – 65.00.

Portrait plate (8¼") with Flow Blue. $65.00 – 75.00.

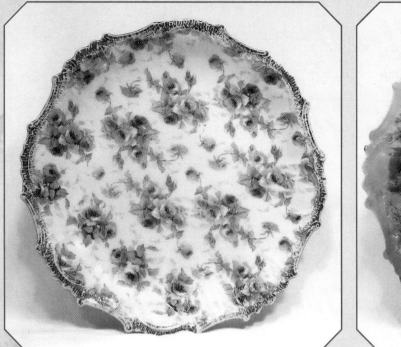

Plate (8¼″) with chintz floral pattern.
$45.00 – 55.00.

Plate (8¼″) with country scene. Reads "Spring."
$45.00 – 55.00.

Plate (7″) with country scene. Reads "Winter."
$45.00 – 55.00.

Platter (13") with flowers. $75.00 – 85.00.

Close up of gold trim on base of platter, often found on Clarus Ware pieces.

Plate (8¼") with portrait. $55.00 – 65.00.

Plate (8¼") with portrait. $55.00 – 65.00.

Plate (8¼") with portrait and Flow Blue.
$65.00 – 75.00.

Plate (9½") with Flow Blue. $55.00 – 65.00.

Plate (8¼") with birds. $45.00 – 55.00.

Plate (8¼") with birds. $45.00 – 55.00.

Plate (8¼") with birds. $45.00 – 55.00.

Plate (8¼") with birds. $45.00 – 55.00.

The following pieces have both the Clarus Ware mark and the Pope-Gosser mark.

Platter (18½" x 13") with pheasant. $155.00 – 175.00.

Plate (6½") with fruit.
$25.00 – 35.00.

Plate (10¼") with figural scene. $75.00 – 85.00.

Cracker bowl (4¼" high) with flowers. $75.00 – 85.00.

This mark, commonly called the unicorn mark, was used from about 1905 to around 1920.

Plate (7") with fruit. $20.00 – 30.00.

Plate (7") with fruit. $20.00 – 30.00.

Plate (7") with fruit. $20.00 – 30.00.

Plate (7") with fruit. $20.00 – 30.00.

Plate (7") with fruit. $20.00 – 30.00.

Plate (7″) with roses. $20.00 – 30.00.

Plate (9¼″) with roses. $30.00 – 40.00.

Calendar plate (8″) dated 1909. $45.00 – 55.00.

Saxon China Company

Saxon China, of Sebring, Ohio, started business about 1900 and operated until about 1929. Saxon China was another one of the many Sebring Brothers companies.

This mark was most likely used from about 1900 to about 1907.

Plate (8½") with fish. $20.00 – 30.00.

Plate (10¼") with fruit. $35.00 – 45.00.

Plate (7¼") with fish. $20.00 – 30.00.

Plate (7½") with country scene. $15.00 – 25.00.

Plate (6¼") with flowers. $15.00 – 25.00.

Plate (9½″) with Flow Blue border. $40.00 – 50.00.

Platter (11½″ x 8″) with Flow Blue.
$135.00 – 155.00.

Plate (8½″) with Flow Blue. $35.00 – 45.00.

Plate (8½") with Flow Blue. $35.00 – 45.00.

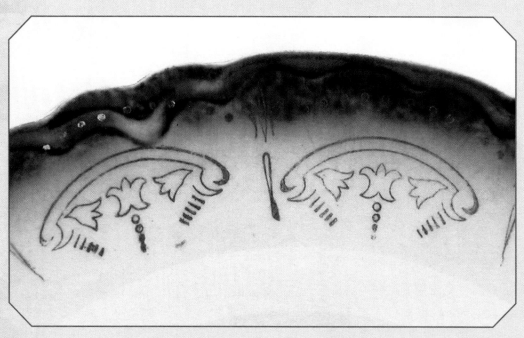

Close up of gold pattern on rim.

Sebring Pottery Company

The company began operation in 1887, when the Sebring brothers bought out the American Pottery Works in East Liverpool, Ohio. The brothers soon acquired land nearby and established the town of Sebring in order to expand their pottery interests, and they moved the company there about 1902. Over the years, the brothers opened numerous potteries in Sebring, and similarities between wares are often noted. The company was in operation until the 1940s. (Other potteries associated with the Sebring Brothers listed in this collection are Crescent China Co., French China Co., Lebeau Porcelaine, Limoges China Co., Ohio China Co., Oliver China Co., Saxon China Co., and Sterling China.)

This mark was used from about 1895 to about 1905.

Plate (12") with elaborate embossing.
$75.00 – 85.00.

Plate (13") with elaborate embossing and Flow Blue.
$115.00 – 125.00.

Bowl (10") with portrait.
$55.00 – 65.00.

Bowl (9¾") with Flow Blue. Reads "DELPH."
$85.00 – 95.00.

Plate (9½") with Flow Blue. $35.00 – 45.00.

Plate (12¾") with elaborate embossing.
$55.00 – 65.00.

Urn (12″) with portrait and pink shading.
$125.00 – 135.00.

Back side of urn.

This mark was used from about 1905 to about 1915.
Reads "KOKUS CHINA."

Plate (8½″) with birds. Decal incorporates artist's signature, Edwin Megargee. $20.00 – 30.00.

Close up of signature on decal.

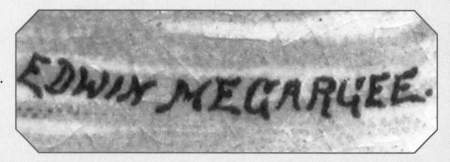

Platter (13¾″ x 10″) with turkeys. $75.00 – 85.00.

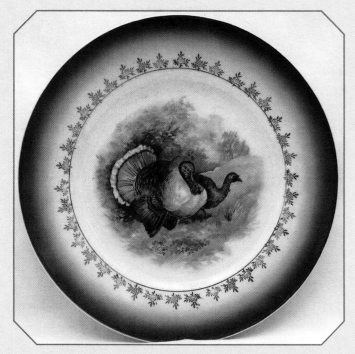

Plate (8½") with turkeys. $20.00 – 30.00.

This mark was used from about 1914 to about 1930. Reads "S. P. CO." "22" indicates the year, 1922.

Platter (13¼" x 10¾") with pheasant. $45.00 – 55.00.

Plate (7″) with pheasant. $15.00 – 25.00.

Plate (7″) with ducks. $15.00 – 25.00.

Plate (7″) with pheasant. $15.00 – 25.00.

Sevres China Company

For a company that was only in business for eight years, there is quite a bit of Sevres on the market. Sevres China Company operated in East Liverpool, Ohio, from 1900 to 1908, and had no relation to the well-known French porcelain company. But, as we often see in early American pottery, the European association was desirable, even to the point of using the French fleur-de-lis mark. Sevres produced a good quality semi-porcelain and a variety of decorative plates. In addition to the "SEVRES" mark, look for the fleur-de-lis mark with the words "MELTON," "GENEVA," or "BERLIN."

This mark was used from 1900 to 1908.

Plate (10½") with colorful leaves. $35.00 – 45.00.

Plate (11") with embossing and roses. $40.00 – 50.00.

Plate (10") with embossed weave pattern.
$40.00 – 50.00.

Bowl (10¼") with cherries. $25.00 – 35.00.

Bowl (10¼") with roses. $25.00 – 35.00.

Bowl (10") with flowers. $20.00 – 30.00.

Plate (10") with minstral. $40.00 – 50.00.

Bowl (9¼") with strawberries. $20.00 – 30.00.

Plate (9¾") with embossing. $35.00 – 45.00.

Souvenir plate (6½") with rose. $15.00 – 25.00.

Souvenir plate (8½") with roses. $20.00 – 30.00.

*Souvenir plate (7¼") with Statue of Liberty.
$25.00 – 35.00.*

Plate (9¼") with Dutch theme. $35.00 – 45.00.

Souvenir plate (6½") with Dutch theme.
$25.00 – 35.00.

Souvenir plate (8¼") with Dutch theme.
$30.00 – 40.00.

Plate (8½") with roses. $30.00 – 40.00.

Plate (8½") with roses. $30.00 – 40.00.

Bowl (11") with roses. $25.00 – 35.00.

Bowl (11") with roses. $25.00 – 35.00.

Platter (12¾" x 9¼") with cherries.
$55.00 – 65.00.

Dish (8½" x 5¾") with roses. $15.00 – 25.00.

Plate (10¼") with roses. $35.00 – 45.00.

Plate (10¼") with roses. $30.00 – 40.00.

Plate (8") with fruit. $30.00 – 40.00.

Plate (8″) with fruit.
$30.00 – 40.00.

Plate (8″) with fruit. $30.00 – 40.00.

Tankard (17″) with minstral.
$155.00 – 175.00.

Plate (8″) with fruit. $30.00 – 40.00.

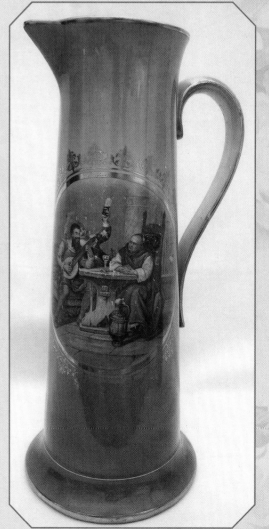

Mugs (5¼") with figural scene. $45.00 – 55.00 each.

Tankard (14") with hand painting.
$165.00 – 185.00.

Mug (5¼") with handpainting. $40.00 – 50.00.

Mug (5¼") with handpainting. $40.00 – 50.00.

Mug (5¼") with handpainting. $40.00 – 50.00.

Mug (5¼") with handpainting. $40.00 – 50.00.

Mug (5¼") with portrait.
$40.00 – 50.00.

Mug (5¼") with fruit.
$35.00 – 45.00.

Plate (11¾") with flowers. $65.00 – 75.00.

Pitcher (9″) with colorful leaves. $75.00 – 85.00.

Vase (10¼″) with Dutch scene.
$95.00 – 115.00.

Pitcher (5″), bird shaped. $45.00 – 55.00.

Shenango China Company

The Shenango China Company began in 1901 in New Castle, Pennsylvania. After some financial difficulty, it reorganized as the Shenango Pottery Co. about 1905, and in 1954, the name was changed to back to Shenango China, Inc. Over the years, the company went through many changes of ownership, and it eventually closed its doors. Shenango has a rich history and is well known for its institutional ware.

This mark was used from about 1905 to about 1910. Reads "SHENANGO POTTERY."

Plate (10") with roses. $50.00 – 60.00.

Smith-Phillips China Company

The Smith Phillips China Co. of East Liverpool, Ohio, began in 1901, when Josiah Smith and William Phillips bought the French China Company. It operated until about 1931.

This mark was used about 1905.

Souvenir plate (7") with portrait of Queen Louise.
$25.00 – 35.00.

Plate (8") with birds. $25.00 – 35.00.

Plate (8″) with birds. $25.00 – 35.00.

Plate (8″) with birds. $25.00 – 35.00.

Plate (8″) with birds. $25.00 – 35.00.

Sterling China

The Sebring brothers built a pottery in Sebring, Ohio, about 1900 and named it Sterling China, with plans for it to produce higher quality wares (porcelain) than their other potteries. This was not profitable, and within a few years, it was producing semi-porcelain and its name had changed to the Limoges China Company. Some authors suggest the Sterling China mark below was the mark used during the short period the company was called Sterling China, but others question this. If the Sterling China mark was only used for a couple of years, then this is definitely not the same mark, because this mark has been found on later pieces. Perhaps it was used before and/or after the company became the Limoges China Co. No porcelain pieces with this mark have been found that would help us identify this as the original mark. My sense is that it is not the original Sterling China mark, but one used later either by the Limoges China Co. or another Sebring family pottery.

DeBolt suggests this mark would have been used from about 1905 to around 1912. Note the decal on the plate on page 230, which reads "Copyright 1909."

Platter (21" x 8¾") with fish. $135.00 – 145.00.

Bowl (9") with monk.
$25.00 – 35.00.

Tankard (13") with hand painting.
$155.00 – 175.00.

Platter (13½" x 10¼") with pheasant.
$75.00 – 85.00.

Platter (14½" x 11¾") with pheasant. $75.00 – 85.00.

Plate (8½") with birds. $20.00 – 30.00.

Plate (8½") with birds. $20.00 – 30.00.

Plate (8½") with birds. $20.00 – 30.00.

Plate (8½") with birds. $20.00 – 30.00.

Plate (8½") with birds. $20.00 – 30.00.

Plate (8½") with birds. $20.00 – 30.00.

Platter (14¼" x 11¾") with pheasant. Decal incorporates artist's signature, R. K. Beck. $65.00 – 75.00.

Plate (9") with birds. R. K. Beck. $20.00 – 30.00.   *Plate (9") with birds. R. K. Beck. $20.00 – 30.00.*

Plate (9") with birds. R. K. Beck. $20.00 – 30.00.

Plate (9") with birds. R. K. Beck. $20.00 – 30.00.

Plate (9") with birds. R. K. Beck. $20.00 – 30.00.

Plate (9″) with birds. R. K. Beck. $20.00 – 30.00.

Plate (9″) with birds. R. K. Beck. $20.00 – 30.00.

Close up of signature on decal.

Plate (7½″) with fish. $20.00 – 30.00.

227

Figural plate (8″) with advertising on back. Reads "Pilgrim Exiles." $20.00 – 25.00.

Plate (6¼″) with advertising (worn away). $20.00 – 30.00.

Plate (10¼″) with flowers and Flow Blue border. $45.00 – 55.00.

Plate (9") with country scene. $40.00 – 50.00.

Plate (9¼") with roses and Flow Blue border. Decal incorporates artist's signature, Peulier. $65.00 – 75.00.

Plate (10") with roses and Flow Blue border. Decal incorporates artist's signature, Peulier. $65.00 – 75.00.

Plate (9¼") with portrait and Flow Blue border.
Decal reads "Copyright 1909 Philip Boileau."
$65.00 – 75.00.

Plate (10½") with flowers and Flow Blue border.
$45.00 – 55.00.

Plate (8½") with ducks and Flow Blue border. Decal
incorporates artist's signature, R. K. Beck.
$35.00 – 45.00.

Bowl (7¾") with flowers and Flow Blue border.
$30.00 – 40.00.

Bowl (9") with country scene and Flow Blue border.
$35.00 – 45.00.

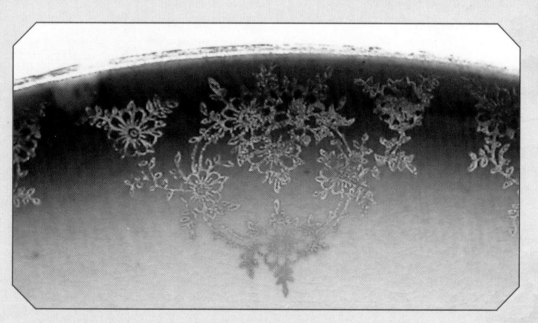

Close-up of gold decoration commonly found on Sterling China pieces.

Close-up of gold decoration commonly found on Sterling China pieces.

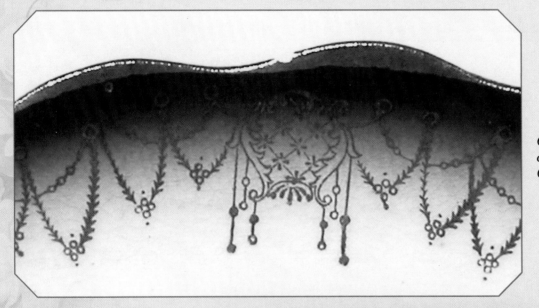

Close-up of gold decoration commonly found on Sterling China pieces.

Close-up of gold decoration commonly found on Sterling China pieces.

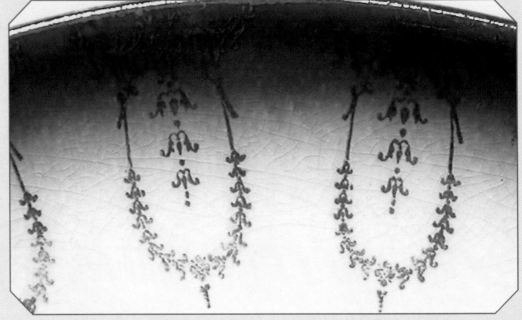

Close-up of gold decoration commonly found on Sterling China pieces.

Close-up of gold decoration commonly found on Sterling China pieces.

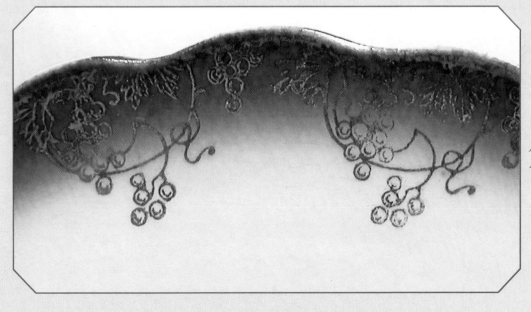

Close-up of gold decoration found on Sterling China pieces.

Steubenville Pottery Company

The Steubenville Pottery Co., of Steubenville, Ohio, operated from 1879 to 1959.

This mark was used from 1890 to about 1904.
Reads "CANTON CHINA."

Bowl (6½") with windmill. $15.00 – 25.00.

Bowl (6½") with boats. $15.00 – 25.00.

Plate (9¼") with McKinley (Govenor of Ohio and U.S. President, assassinated in 1901).
$35.00 – 45.00.

This mark was used from about 1910 to about 1920. It is plentiful, and often assumed to be French or Austrian because of its elaborate decoration and interesting shapes. Pieces would be marked with the words "Empire China" within a wreath, and would be stamped with a number. Empire China represents a wonderful collectible and a good value.

Plate (10½") with roses. Decal incorporates artist's signature, E. Muller. #834. $45.00 – 55.00.

Close up of signature on decal.

Plate (9½") with portrait of George Washington. #4277. $40.00 – 50.00.

Plate (9½") with portrait. #361. $65.00 – 75.00.

Bowl (10¾") with portrait. #336. $35.00 – 45.00.   *Bowl (10¼") with portrait. #4047. $55.00 – 65.00.*

Compote (10" across x 3" high) with roses. #4064. $55.00 – 65.00.

Inside view of preceding item.

Plate (10½") with American History theme. Reads "WASHINGTON CROSSING THE DELAWARE." #4061. $65.00 – 75.00.

Plate (10½") with hunt scene. #4057. $45.00 – 55.00.

Plate (10½") with figural scene. #862
$45.00 – 55.00.

Plate (10½") with figural scene. Also #862.
$45.00 – 55.00.

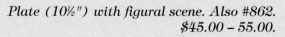

Plate (10½") with cherub. Number is unreadable.
$45.00 – 55.00.

Plate (10½") with portrait. Number is unreadable.
$65.00 – 75.00.

Bowl (10½") with roses. #909. $35.00 – 45.00.

Plate (10½") with figural scene. #849.
$65.00 – 75.00.

Plate (9¾") with figural scene. #943. $45.00 – 55.00.

Plate (10") with figural scene. #944. $45.00 – 55.00.

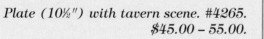

Plate (10½") with tavern scene. #4265.
$45.00 – 55.00.

Plate (10") with figural scene. #948.
$45.00 – 55.00.

242

Plate (10") with figural scene. #945.
$45.00 – 55.00.

Plate (10") with figural scene. Also #945.
$45.00 – 55.00.

Plate (10½") with portrait. #682.
$65.00 – 75.00.

Plate (10½") with portrait of George Washington.
#4038. $65.00 – 75.00.

Plate (10½") with portrait. #879. $65.00 – 75.00.

Plate (9¾") with country scene. Decal reads "Summer."
#857. $40.00 – 50.00.

Plate (9½") with portrait of Queen Louise. #499.
$55.00 – 65.00.

Pitcher (7") with grapes. #4800. $65.00 – 75.00.

Pitcher (6½") with grapes. #4229. $65.00 – 75.00.
From the collection of Faye Lyon.

Dish (12¼" x 5¾") with grapes. #4229. $45.00 – 55.00.

Vase (11") with grapes. #4229.
$85.00 – 95.00.

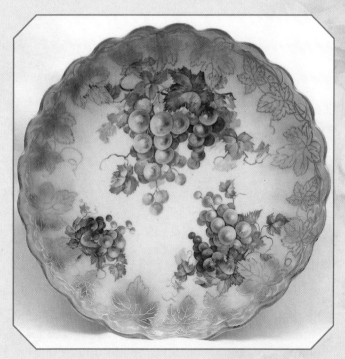

Plate (10½") with grapes. #4229. $45.00 – 55.00.

Bowl (10½") with grapes. #4229.
$45.00 – 55.00.

This mark was used from about 1910 to about
1920. Reads "STEUBENVILLE CHINA."

Bowl (10½") with grapes, matte finish. #4200.
$35.00 – 45.00.

Taylor, Smith & Taylor Company

The Taylor, Smith & Taylor Co. began around the turn of the century, with an office in East Liverpool and a factory across the Ohio River, in West Virginia. In 1972, it was acquired by Anchor Hocking, and production ceased in 1981.

This TST mark with the winged lion was used from 1901 to about 1915.

Plate (9¾") with roses. $35.00 – 45.00.

Plate (9") with portrait. Decal incorporates artist's signature, Vittori. $55.00 – 65.00.

This mark is a variation of the preceding mark and was used about the same time.

Souvenir plate (7½") with homestead. Reads "THE OLD McKINLEY HOME LISBON, OHIO." $25.00 – 35.00.

Plate (10") with fruit. $40.00 – 50.00.

This mark was used from 1908 to about 1915.

Plate (9¼") with roses. $40.00 – 50.00.

Plate (9") with dog, $45.00 – 55.00.

Plate (9½") with cardinal. $50.00 – 60.00.

Plate (9¾") with dog.
$45.00 – 55.00.

Plate (9") with roses. $35.00 – 45.00.

Plate (9¼") with roses. $40.00 – 50.00.

Plate (9¼") with roses. Decal incorporates artist's signature, Guyeau. $35.00 – 45.00.

Plate (9½") with chestnuts. Decal incorporates artist's signature, R.K. Beck. $55.00 – 65.00.

Plate (9½") with corn. Decal incorporates artist's signature, R. K. Beck. $55.00 – 65.00.

Plate (8¼") with friar. Decal reads "Commend Married Life to Everyone But Keep Thyself a Bachelor." $25.00 – 35.00.

Plate (8") with minstral. Decal reads "MUSIC HATH CHARMS." $25.00 – 35.00.

Advertising plate (6") with violets. $25.00 – 35.00.

Tankard (13½″) with monk. $155.00 – 175.00.

Mugs (4¾″) with monk. $45.00 – 55.00 each.

Pitcher (6¾″) with fruit. $65.00 – 75.00.

Pitcher (6¾") with fruit. $65.00 – 75.00.

Pitcher (6¾") with fruit. $65.00 – 75.00.

This mark was used from about 1910 to about 1920.
Reads "T S T LATONA CHINA."

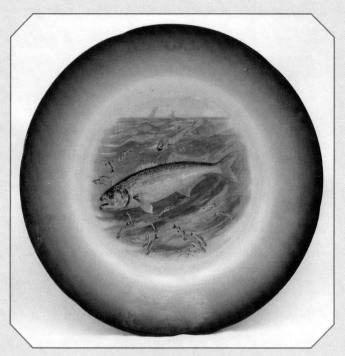

Plate (9¾") with fish. Decal incorporates artist's signature, R. K. Beck. $25.00 – 35.00.

Plate (9¾") with fish. Decal incorporates artist's signature, R. K. Beck. $25.00 – 35.00.

Plate (9¾") with fish. Decal incorporates artist's signature, R. K. Beck. $25.00 – 35.00.

Close-up of signature on decal.

C. C. Thompson Pottery Company

The C.C. Thompson Pottery Company, of East Liverpool, Ohio, began in 1868 as Thompson and Herbert. By 1870, it was C.C. Thompson and Company, and, finally, in 1889 it became the C.C. Thompson Pottery Company. It closed in 1938.

This mark is common and dates from about 1905 to about 1930.

Bowl (9¼") with bird. $15.00 – 25.00.

Plate (10¼") with roses. $20.00 – 30.00.

Bowl (9¼") with bird. $15.00 – 25.00.

Bowl (10") with roses. $15.00 – 25.00.

Bowl (9¾") with ship. $15.00 – 25.00.

Bowl (9") with bird. $15.00 – 25.00.

Platter (15½" x 11¼") with roses. $55.00 – 65.00.

Trenle China Company

The East End Pottery Company became the Trenle China Co. about 1910. In 1937, its name changed to the Trenle, Blake China Company. It remained in business until 1966.

This mark was used from about 1910 to about 1917.

Plate (9") with advertising. $30.00 – 40.00.

United States Pottery Company

The United States Pottery Company of Wellsville, Ohio, began in 1899. In 1900, the United States Pottery Company joined with five other potteries in the area to form the East Liverpool Potteries Company. In 1903, four of the potteries dropped out, leaving only the United States Pottery Company and Globe Pottery until 1907, when the East Liverpool Potteries Company ended. The United States Pottery Co. continued to use marks that included the East Liverpool Potteries Company name (or initials) until it closed around 1930.

This mark was used about 1899.
(Mark retouched for clarity.)

Plate (7½") with fruit. $20.00 – 30.00.

Plate (8¾") with advertising. $25.00 – 35.00.

Plate (12½") with fruit. $35.00 – 45.00.

Plate (9¼") with cherries. $25.00 – 35.00.

Plate (6½") with village scene. $15.00 – 25.00.

Warner–Keffer China Company

The Sevres China Co., of East Liverpool, Ohio, became the Warner-Keffer China Co. in 1908 and operated until 1911.

This mark was used from about 1908 to about 1911. Reads "W. K. C. CO. E. L. O."

Tankard (13″) with fruit. $165.00 – 185.00.

Warwick China Company

The Warwick China Company of Wheeling, West Virginia, operated from 1887 to 1951 and produced hotel ware, and high quality dinnerware as well as a line of decorative pieces marked "IOGA." These "IOGA" pieces are widely sought after and bring premium prices, most of which are above the price range of this collection.

This mark was used between 1898 and about 1910.

Plate (12") with roses. $75.00 – 85.00.

Plate (12") with roses. $75.00 – 85.00.

Plate (11") with flowers. $45.00 – 55.00.

Plate (10") with roses. $45.00 – 55.00.

Plate (8¼") with flowers. $45.00 – 55.00.

Dish (11" x 5¼") with roses. $20.00 – 30.00.

Dish (11" x 5½") with flowers.
$55.00 – 65.00.

Tray (11½" x 7½") with flowers.
$75.00 – 85.00.

Pitcher (6¾") with flowers
$125.00 – 155.00.

Pitcher (4½") with flowers.
$75.00 – 85.00.

Pitcher (6½") with flowers.
$135.00 – 155.00.

Jardinière (8" high x 9½" across) with embossing.
$195.00 – 255.00.

This *"IOGA" mark was used from about 1900 to about 1915 and has been featured in several books.*

Plate (10¼") with bulldog. Reads "CHAMPION RODNEY STONE." $115.00 – 125.00.

Plate (9½") with monk. $85.00 – 95.00.

Wellsville China Company

The Wellsville China Company began in about 1902, when the Pioneer Pottery Company of Wellsville, Ohio, reorganized as a result of financial difficulties. About 1933, it began producing institutional wares, and was taken over in 1959 by the Sterling China Co. of Wellsville, Ohio.

This mark was used from about 1910 to about 1920.

Dish (13" x 6") with flowers. $25.00 – 35.00.

Dish (13" x 6") with flowers. $25.00 – 35.00.

Dish (13" x 6") with flowers. $25.00 – 35.00.

Dish (13" x 6") with flowers. $25.00 – 35.00.

Dish (13" x 6") with flowers. $25.00 – 35.00.

Dish (9" x 5") with flowers.
$25.00 – 35.00.

Bowl (9") with roses.
$15.00 – 20.00.

Pitcher (10¼") with roses.
$125.00 – 155.00.

Wheeling Pottery Company

The Wheeling Pottery Company, of Wheeling, West Virginia, began operation in 1879. In 1887, the La Belle Pottery was formed under the same management, and in 1889, the two companies were combined. Over the years, the company formed several other potteries, and in 1903, all of its potteries were combined and its name changed to the Wheeling Potteries Company. Of special interest is its La Belle China Flow Blue. Prices for some of these patterns are through the roof. I recently saw a La Belle China Flow Blue chocolate pot sell for over $700, and a demitasse cup and saucer sell for over $500. Collecting La Belle Flow Blue is serious business. Fortunately, La Belle made beautiful, decorative pieces that are not Flow Blue, so the rest of us can afford them. Wheeling Potteries operated until about 1909.

This La Belle China mark was used from 1893 to about 1905, by the La Belle Pottery.

Plate (11¼") with strawberries and Flow Blue border.
$125.00 – 155.00.

Plate (12") with layered effect.
$55.00 – 65.00.

Dish (9¼") with handle.
$55.00 – 65.00.

Pitcher/ewer (10½") with flowers.
$125.00 – 145.00.

Plate (12½") with flowers. $45.00 – 55.00.

Platter (13"x 9¾") with roses. $75.00 – 85.00.

Plate (8½") with hand painted accents.
$55.00 – 65.00. From the collection of Faye Lyon.

Plate (9") with birds. $20.00 – 30.00.

Plate (9") with deer. $20.00 – 30.00.

Plate (10") with boar. $25.00 – 35.00.

Plate (10") with deer. $25.00 – 35.00.

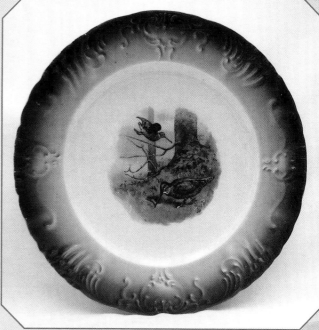

Plate (10") with birds. $25.00 – 35.00.

Plate (10") with birds. $25.00 – 35.00.

Plate (10") with rabbits. $25.00 – 35.00.

**This mark was used from 1893 to about 1904,
by the La Belle Pottery factory.**

Plate (12") with flowers. $50.00 – 60.00.

This mark was used from 1894 to possibly as late as 1909, by the La Belle Pottery factory.

Jardinière (15" high x 13½" across) with flowers. $135.00 – 155.00.

This mark was used from about 1904 to about 1909, by the La Belle Pottery factory. (Mark was retouched for clarity.)

Pitcher/coffee pot (7½") with flowers.
$125.00 – 145.00.

Opposite side.

This mark was used about 1900. Reads "IMPERIAL PORCELAIN WARRANTED."

Plate (8½″) with fish. $20.00 – 30.00.

Plate (8½″) with fish.
$20.00 – 30.00.

This mark was used about 1903 to about 1909 at the Avon pottery of Tiltonsville, Ohio, one of the Wheeling family of potteries. Avon was formerly Vance Faience Co., before becoming part of Wheeling.

Mug (5¼″) with portrait. $55.00 – 65.00.

This mark was used from about 1906 to about 1909. Reads "Bonita."

Plate (10″) with portrait. $45.00 – 55.00.

Wick China Company

The Wick China Company, of Kittanning, Pennsylvania, operated from 1889 to about 1905, when it became the Pennsylvania China Company.

This mark was used about 1900. Reads "Aurora China."

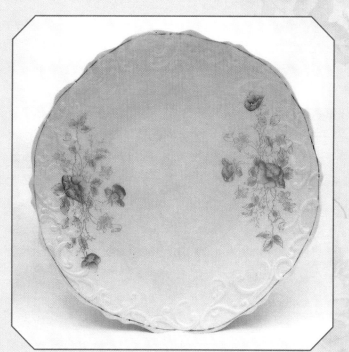

Plate (10¼") with flowers. $30.00 – 40.00.
From the collection of Faye Lyon.

Dish (14" x 10¼") with flowers. $55.00 – 65.00.
From the collection of Faye Lyon.

Willets Manufacturing Company

The Willets Manufacturing Co. operated in Trenton, New Jersey, from 1879 to about 1909. It is especially noted for its fine line of Belleek wares, which are widely collected and are priced beyond the range of this collection.

This mark was used about 1890. Reads
"W. M. CO. SEMI PORCELAIN."

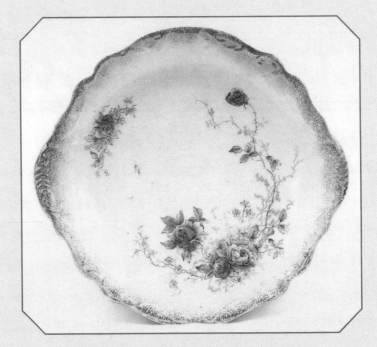

Plate (11") with hand painted accents.
$35.00 – 45.00.

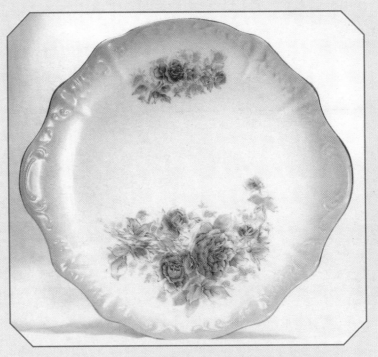

Plate (11") with hand painted accents.
$35.00 – 45.00.

H. R. Wyllie China Company

The H. R. Wyllie China Company began in Huntington, West Virginia, and produced semi-porcelain from about 1910 until the late 1920s.

This mark was used from about 1910 to about 1920, and is commonly found on Flow Blue pieces.

Bowl (9½″) with roses. $20.00 – 30.00.

Bowl (9½″) with roses. $20.00 – 30.00.

Plate (9½″) with roses. $25.00 – 35.00.

Bowl (9") with roses and Flow Blue border.
$25.00 – 35.00.

Platter (12¾" x 9¾") with roses and Flow Blue border.
$85.00 – 95.00.

Plate (9½") with fruit. $35.00 – 45.00.

Plate (10¾") with portrait. $35.00 – 45.00.

Confusing Marks

In the early days of pottery making in America, European wares were considered superior in quality. To overcome this impediment to sales, some American potteries used names or marks that might easily be confused with foreign marks. Here are some marks that might confuse you as you collect.

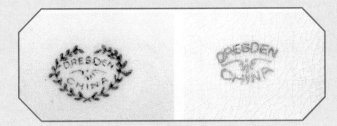

American Dresden China Co. East
Liverpool, Ohio

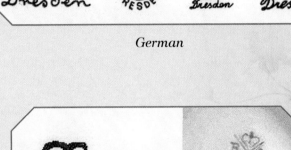

German

American
Sevres China Co. East
Liverpool, Ohio

French
There are several variations of these marks.

American
Limoges China Co. East
Liverpool, Ohio

French

The Plate is Grazing

None of us knows everything about pottery, so mistakes are bound to happen when describing a piece to sell. Sometimes it's a typo, sometimes we get confused, and sometimes we just stretch it a bit. Here is a collection of questionable comments by sellers from online auctions that is sure to make you chuckle.

"The plate suffers from grazing" (Meaning: "The plate has crazing.")

"semi-virtuous bowl" (Meaning: "semi-vitreous bowl.")

"has self-healed lines" (Meaning: "it has cracks.")

"The platter has three chips and two hairlines and is in great condition." (Meaning: "other than all that damage.")

"The plate has a 1" hairline on the back, but no chips or cracks." (Meaning: "I'm not counting a hairline as a crack.)"

"The crack may just be in the glaze, I can't tell." (Meaning: "I can't bring myself to call it a crack.")

"There are a few age cracks, but no chips or cracks." (Meaning: "Age cracks don't count, do they?")

"Although the handle is broken, there are no chips or cracks." (Meaning: " 'Broken' is its own category of damage.")

"This piece is absolutely flawless, except the one area where it looks like four of the applied decorations on the top are missing." (Meaning: "It is far from flawless.)"

"looks to have a hairline crack in the bottom; I have found out dealing with antiques that cracks sometimes increase the value of an antique." (Meaning: "I'll believe anything.")

"I was told that this plate is either from 1896, 1906, or 1916, due to the fact that there are six roses in the design, which (supposedly) represents the last digit in the year it was manufactured." (Meaning: "give or take 20 years.")

"In the upper left, it looks as if it tried to chip, but the green color remains, so I guess it's not really a chip." (Meaning: "If I don't call it a chip, it's not a chip.")

"It is in wonderful condition, with no chips or cracks; the back rim has a few tiny chips on the base." (Meaning: "Chips on the back don't count.")

"There are no chips or cracks other than the crazing, but it does have a few fleabites." (Meaning: "Fleabites don't count.")

Bibliography

Altman, Seymour and Violet. *The Book of Buffalo Pottery*. New York, NY: Crown Publishers Inc., 1969.

Barber, Edwin Atlee. T*he Pottery and Porcelain of the United States*. NewYork: G. P. Putnam's Sons, 1909 and *Marks of American Potters, Philadelphia: Patterson and White,* 1904, reprinted in one volume. New York: J. & J. Publishing, 1976.

Buys, Susan and Oakley, Victoria. *The Conservation and Restoration of Ceramics.* Bury St Edmunds, Suffolk: St Edmundsbury Press Ltd., 1999.

Cunningham, Jo. *The Collector's Encyclopedia of American Dinnerware*. Paducah, KY: Collector Books, 1982.

____. *Homer Laughlin, A Giant Among Dishes: 1873-1939*. Atglen, PA: Schiffer Publishing Ltd., 1998.

DeBolt, Gerald. *Dictionary of American Pottery Marks*. Paducah, KY: Collector Books, 1994.

Duke, Harvey. *Official Price Guide to Pottery and Porcelain*, 8th edition. New York, NY: House of Collectibles, 1995.

Earle, Alice Morse. "A China Hunter in New England." *Scribner's Magazine,* September 1891. New York, NY: Charles Scribner's Sons.

Gaston, Mary Frank. *Collector's Encyclopedia of Knowles, Taylor & Knowles China*. Paducah, KY: Collector Books, 1996.

Hawley, Carrie M. "American Pottery," *The Midland Monthly,* Vol. 2, No. 1, July 1894 Des Moines, IA: Kenyon's Press.

Jackson, Albert and Day, David. *Care and Repair of Antiques and Collectables*. London, England: Harper Collins Publishers, 1998.

Jasper, Joanne. *The Collector's Encyclopedia of Homer Laughlin China*. Paducah, KY: Collector Books, 1995.

____.*Turn of the Century American Dinnerware, 1880s to 1920s*. Paducah, KY: Collector Books, 1996.

Kearns, Timothy J. *Knowles, Taylor & Knowles American Bone China*. Atglen, PA: Schiffer Publishing Ltd., 1994.

Kovel, Ralph and Terry. *Kovels' New Dictionary of Marks*. New York, NY: Crown Publishers Inc., 1985.

Lehner, Lois. *Complete Book of American Kitchen and Dinner Wares*. Des Moines, IA: Wallace-Homestead Book Co., 1980.

____. *U.S. Marks on Pottery, Porcelain and Clay*. Paducah, KY: Collector Books, 1988.

Limoges, Raymonde. *American Limoges Identification & Value Guide*. Paducah, KY: Collector Books, 1996.

Miller, Judith. *Care and Repair of Everyday Treasures*. Pleasantville, N. Y.: The Reader's Digest Association Inc., 1997.

Rader, John R., Sr. *Warwick China*. Atglen, PA: Schiffer Publishing Ltd., 2000.

Recollecting Pope-Gosser. Coshocton, Ohio: The Johnson-Humrickhouse Museum, 2000.

Schroeder, Joseph J., Jr., Editor. *Sears, Roebuck & Co. 1908 Catalogue No. 117, Reproduction*. Northfield, IL: Digest Books Inc., 1971.

About the Author

Tom and Jeanie Wilby

Born in Kansas, Jeanie grew up in St. Louis, Missouri. In 1972, she moved to South Florida, where she taught in the Broward County Public School System. In 1996, she and her husband, Tom, sold their home and business and began a year-long journey across the United States in an RV. It was during this period that she began to take an interest in American pottery.

In 1997, Jeanie and Tom returned to Florida and settled near Orlando, in the historic community of Enterprise. She teaches Exceptional Student Education at Freedom Elementary School in Deland, Florida. She holds a Bachelor's Degree from Southeast Missouri State University in Cape Girardeau, Missouri, and a Master's Degree from Florida International University in Miami, Florida.

Besides collecting, Jeanie enjoys buying and selling on eBay under the username *idodishes*. You can reach her at *idodishes@wilby.name*.

Index

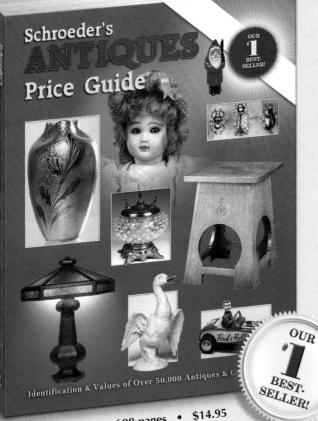